Delicate

New Food Culture

gestalten

Christopher Schweiger, Peter Fehringer

TONGUES
Vienna, Austria (2010)

TONGUES is a delicatessen—and a record shop. This unusual combination, created by Christopher Schweiger and Peter Fehringer, is not the only thing that makes Tongues unique; their focus on the finest food in Austria is exemplary. Only products that are locally sourced and crafted with artisan care make it to the shop; salt from the Austrian Alps, handmade bread from the Waldviertel, and milk from Styrian cows that are sustainably raised in the herb-filled pastures of the Karnerviertel are just some of the products they carry.

Photo: Christiano Tekirdali, www.christiano.at

THE NEW DEAL

Personal relationships with the farmers they buy from, business models that involve working together with family or friends to get the job done, and priorities that place importance on trust: all these elements make today's independent food stores and producers feel like modern-day mom and pop enterprises — with a quirky twist. The clever inventiveness of these businesses produces unique products that reflect the personal stories and values of their creators. Instead of one-stop shopping at megastores, customers are seeking out stores and producers who are masters of their craft, part of a sustainable chain of production, and who deliver a distinct product.

Matt Higgins, Keith Gehrke

Coava Roastery and Coffee Bar
Portland, USA

Coava is a family of hard working people who love coffee. Matt Higgins and Keith Gehrke turned their dreams into a coffee roastery and brew bar that is committed to providing the best quality coffee that focuses on single origin beans and optimum brewing techniques, and on bringing people together.

Photo: Jelani Memory

Opposite page & right

Stumptown Coffee Roasters
Duane Sorenson

Manhattan Café in the Ace Hotel Lobby
New York, USA (2009)

Duane Sorenson opened his only Stumptown Coffee Roasters café in New York on Labor Day, 2009. This new location, in the lobby of the Ace Hotel, lets people from all over the world try its high quality coffee.

Photo: Luke Dirks

Stumptown Coffee Roasters
Duane Sorenson

Red Hook Brew Bar
Brooklyn, USA (2009)

The Red Hook Brew Bar is dedicated to teaching coffee lovers the correct way to brew coffee using different brewing methods. The brew bar also hosts regular cuppings and tastings.

Photo: Luke Dirks

Stumptown Coffee Roasters
Duane Sorenson

Roastery in Portland, Oregon
Portland, USA (1999)

We at Stumptown travel worldwide because
we are committed to sourcing and roasting the
best coffees available anywhere. Along the way,
we search for partnerships with farms to share
in a belief that working together year after year
results in the highest level of quality.

Photo: Benji Wagner

Frank Falcinelli, Frank Castronovo, Tony Durazzo, Travis Kauffman

Prime Meats
Brooklyn, USA (2008)

Prime Meats, created by Frank Falcinelli, Frank Castronovo, Tony Durazzo, and Travis Kauffman, is a farm-to-table restaurant created in the spirit of the inns and dining rooms found in New York at the turn of the twentieth century. Although Prime Meats is influenced by Germanic alpine cuisine, its menu also pays tribute to the American artisan movement by featuring local and fresh ingredients that are prepared simply and honestly. The result is fare that is as rustic and warm as the reclaimed leather benches that line its dining room walls.

Photo: All images by Travis Lee Kauffman

Frank Falcinelli, Frank Castronovo, Tony Durazzo, Travis Kauffman

Prime Meats
Brooklyn, USA (2008)

Christoph Keller

Edelobstbrennerei Stählemühle
Eigeltingen im Hegau, Germany (2006)

In 2004, after Christoph Keller sold his art publishing house to a new owner, he moved with his family to a property in Lake Constance called Stählemühle. In addition to a sanctuary for endangered animals, he has operated the Edelobstbrennerei Stählemühle, with his wife, Christine Bohacker, since 2006. The idea for this project is that a sustainable and organic operation can be achieved on one tiny farm with only a small amount of land, a lot of know-how, and the work of four hands. The distillery, which produces fruit brandies in small, high-quality batches, has been named one of the top ten distilleries in the world. In addition to this distinction, Stählemühle has been the recipient of over 160 other awards including the prestigious "Brandy of the Year 2011," the "Golden shot glass" in Austria, and in 2010 it was given the top award by the German Agricultural Society (DLG). The distillery, which only produces 1500 bottles per year, sells to top restaurants such as Brenner's Park Hotel in Baden-Baden and Reinstoff in Berlin, as well as the First Class Lounge of Lufthansa, and the German Bank.

Photo: All images by Bernd Kammerer
Additional credits: Renovation of office buildings and mills by SAB Architekten, Basel, and e15, Frankfurt am Main/Oberursel; 2010 renovation of the distillery, tasting house, and cellar by e15

Christoph Keller

Edelobstbrennerei Stählemühle

Eigeltingen im Hegau, Germany (2006)

OOS

La Galerie du Vin
Zurich, Switzerland (2010)

La Galerie du Vin is a shop as well as a wine tasting and seminar venue. The intent of the interior, designed by the Swiss architecture firm OOS, is to present a landscape built by wine cases in which high-quality wines are paired with their cases; some 1,500 unbranded wine cases from the Bordeaux region cover the entire room, acting as architectural elements and as part of the furniture. Arranged in a grid pattern, they serve as a platform for about 570 wines, books, seating areas, and illuminated table display cabinets. The wines are spatially divided into various groupings, revealing histories, cultures, and landscapes. The reception counter, located in the middle of the room, is equipped for wine consultation. Its violet and ruby colors provide a contrast to the wood of the wine cases. Across from the showroom is a sitting room with a small kitchen. This section is used as the reception room for wine tastings and seminars.

Client: Albert Reichmuth AG
Photo: Christine Müller, www.wehrlimueller.ch

Daniel Bixel

Bixels
Berlin, Germany (2010)

Bixels, a baked potato deli founded by Daniel
Bixel, devotes hours to baking locally and organically grown potatoes in a vintage oven. The result is a perfectly baked potato (crispy on the out-
side and fluffy on the inside) that is then mashed
with butter and cheese and filled with a choice
of ingredients, including goat cheese, Argentine
beef, spinach, pomegranate walnut sauce, sum-
mer veggies, honey carrots, spinach sauce, tuna,
carrot apple salad, chicken, and walnuts.

Photo: Gregor Schmidt

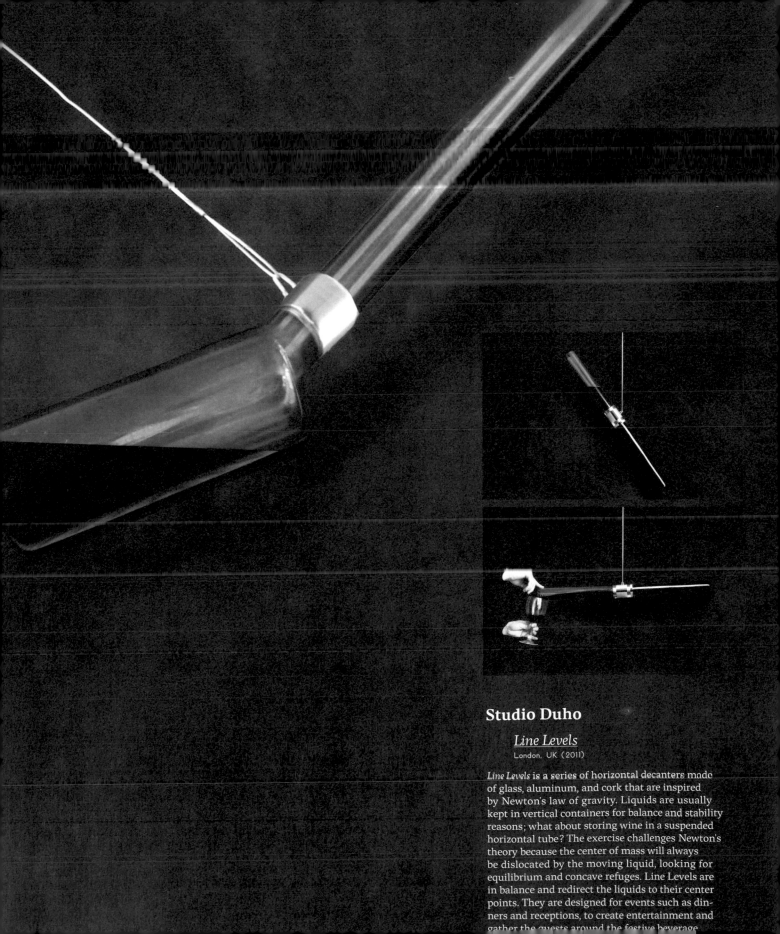

Studio Duho

Line Levels
London, UK (2011)

Line Levels is a series of horizontal decanters made of glass, aluminum, and cork that are inspired by Newton's law of gravity. Liquids are usually kept in vertical containers for balance and stability reasons; what about storing wine in a suspended horizontal tube? The exercise challenges Newton's theory because the center of mass will always be dislocated by the moving liquid, looking for equilibrium and concave refuges. Line Levels are in balance and redirect the liquids to their center points. They are designed for events such as dinners and receptions, to create entertainment and gather the guests around the festive beverage.

Kochhaus

Kochhaus Schöneberg

Berlin, Germany (2010)

Kochhaus is a new concept in the field of food and cooking; roughly sixteen tables are placed throughout the store, each containing the organic fresh and dry ingredients for a complete meal. Meals change regularly so that customers can always try something new and find everything they need in one place. Meal sizes are customized to accommodate the number of diners, making it easy to plan a small but delicious meal for two or an elaborate dinner party. A recipe card with photographs accompanies each meal.

Architecture & design: bfs d flachsbarth schultz
Photo: Annette Kisling

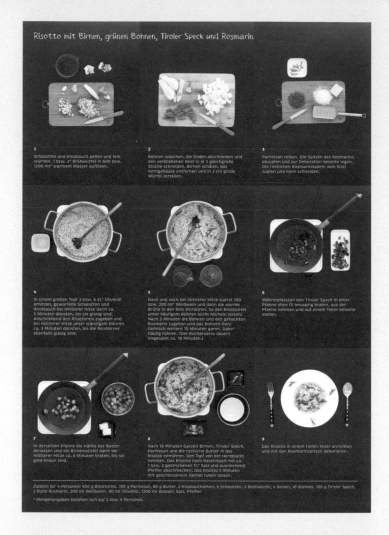

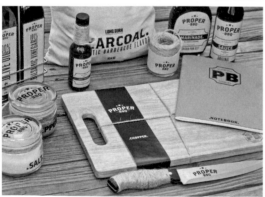

Tom Hayes

Proper BBQ
Savannah, USA (2011)

Proper BBQ allows fine gentlemen to get messy. This range of products is essential for the BBQ-mad or the lavish-but-messy hungry man. Designed with a big, bold, punchy flavor in mind, each product allows the user to get crazy and splash some charisma into their food.

Photo: Tom Hayes

Freshthrills
John Merlino & Kingsley Harris

Motorman Chocolate Lager
Brooklyn, USA (2010)

The inspiration for the branding of this beer, sent as a self-promotional holiday gift, was found on Brooklyn's waterfront. The Motorman was the title of Brooklyn's trolley engineers during the early 1900s. Their resourcefulness as electrical maintenance men, and conductors of the trolleys meant that their jobs were tough but respectable, echoing the way Freshthrills approaches its own work. To push the concept further, the Motorman's Decree was developed. This set of guidelines was imprinted on coasters and brought in a little humor to the project while also making it into a useful keepsake.

Photo: Kingsley Harris & John Merlino

Lindy & Grundy's Meats

Butcher Shop
Los Angeles, USA (2011)

Sustainable butcher shops practice true nose-to-tail butchering, a technique that uses the whole animal and produces very little waste. Lindy & Grundy's Meats does just that and considers themselves an old-fashioned butcher shop. The small family farms they work with are old-fashioned too; their animals are never given antibiotics or hormones and the grass they eat is never treated with pesticides or herbicides. Working with local ranchers located within 150 miles of their Los Angeles shop guarantees that Lindy & Grundy's strict standards are maintained. Eating food that is locally grown allows for 100% traceability and supports local economies and communities.

Photo: Jennifer May, www.jennifermay.com

Dreamtime Australia
Michael McCann

Victor Churchill
Sydney, Australia (2009)

The original Churchill's butcher shop, located
on Queen Street in Woollahra, was founded in
1876 by James Churchill. Victor and Anthony
Puharich, the founders of Vic's Premium Quality Meat (Australia's largest meat wholesaler of
premium meats) became the fourth owners of
the butcher shop and hired Michael McCann of
Dreamtime Australia to design a store unlike
any other butcher shop in Australia. Rich timber-
paneled walls, beamed ceilings, Italian Cala-
catta marble floor, Himalayan salt brick walls,
and floor-to-ceiling glass refrigerated spaces
transformed the space of Victor Churchill from
a traditional butcher shop with refrigerated cabinets and parsley-dressed meats into an award-
winning store infused with European style.

Client: Vic's Premium Quality Meat
Photo: Paul Gosney

Tomás Alonso

Licor Cafe
Vigo, Spain and London, UK (2010)

Licor Cafe is homemade with care by Enrique Alonso in Vigo, Spain, using a traditional recipe from Galicia. Its ingredients consist of Orujo, coffee beans, and sugar. Orujo, also known as _aguardiente_ (burning water), is made locally in many villages of the region, contains over 50% alcohol, and should be served cold. Tomás Alonso designed this set for the beverage his dad has been making for many years. One bottle and five glasses serve five friends around a table. Each glass holds the same quantity of Licor Cafe.

Photo: Cemal Okten

Mamecha
Hidetoshi Toya

Green Tea Café Mamecha
Berlin, Germany (2010)

A cafe in Berlin that serves authentic Japanese tea and food. The menu changes frequently, while seasonal teas match the weather and the mood.

Photo: Satoshi Kinugawa

Atelier Waechter
Ben Waechter

J-Tea
Eugene, USA (2010)

J-Tea International, an importer and seller of Taiwanese oolong teas, wanted to gracefully transform an existing single family house into a retail space making as few changes as possible. The resulting transformation, designed by Atelier Waechter, is composed of three primary elements: an entry canopy, porch, and tea walls. The canopy engages pedestrian and vehicular traffic and gives the former house a commercial scale while creating an airy and glowing entry court for outdoor seating. The white powder-coated aluminum louvers of the canopy stand out against the more subdued galvanized steel structure, appearing to float because they are placed below the support structure. The eye is drawn into the tea room by the porch, which creates an aperture that frames the interior space as if it

were a stage. The porch walls, floor, and roof are made from a relatively thin beam laminated with Port Orford Cedar glue. Two concrete stem walls and cantilevers lightly support the porch at each end, emphasizing the entry threshold. A contained ring around a central tea bar is formed by the tea walls, creating a calm and quiet room, which heightens the senses for smelling and tasting the tea. The tea walls are composed of a grid of maple plywood that circumscribes the room and incorporates window openings for a continuous appearance. The grid of shelves is filled with richly colored and textured merchandise that creates a variegated pattern.

Client: J-Tea International
Photo: Sally Schoolmaster

EventArchitectuur
Paul Kuipers & Herman Verkerk

Warmoesmarkt
Amsterdam, Netherlands (2008)

Warmoesmarkt, designed by EventArchitectuur, is a food market in Amsterdam offering regional products such as vegetables, fruits, milk, cheese, jams, and mustards, as well as cooking workshops. The courtyard features a landscaped, a relaxation area with greenhouses for growing tomatoes, zucchini, eggplants, and herbs, and an aviary and fountain.

Client: Piet Hekker
Photo: Vincent Zedelius
Additional credits: Graphics by Lesley Moore,
Wall drawings in relaxation room by Peter Moeller

Rick's Picks
Rick Field

Rick's Picks Sampler
New York, USA (2004)

Rick's Picks fall into three categories of delight-fully named pickles: you've got your sweet pickles, like the Pepi Pep Peps and Phat Beets; the savory varieties, such as the Windy City Wasabeans and Slices of Life; and the spicy numbers, like Heat Seekers and Spears of Influence. The Rick's Picks Sampler lets both the indecisive and the pickle enthusiast test nine varieties of Rick's Picks. They also throw in some Handy Corn, their limited-edition corn relish, as a bonus as well as a recipe card filled with delicious ways to add Rick's Picks to any menu.

Brand design: Stiletto NYC
Photo: Tom Monaghan

Below

Bompas & Parr

Occult Jam
London, UK (2010)

When asked to come up with a food-based response to *The Surreal House*, an exhibit at London's Barbican Art Gallery, Bompas & Parr conceived of the idea for *Occult Jam*. Convinced that jam could be transformed into a surreal object, they preserved Princess Diana's hair as well as sand from the Great Pyramid.

Client: Barbican Art Gallery
Photo: Ann Charlott Ommedal

Above

Brooklyn Soda Works
Brooklyn, USA (2010)

It was an artist and a chemist who joined forces to create Brooklyn Soda Works, a Brooklyn-based soda company. The palette used to create these unconventional soda flavors consists of freshly squeezed juices from seasonal (and local) fruits and herbs to create flavor combinations such as Concord Grape & Fennel Seed, and Strawberry, Hops & Pink Peppercorn.

Design: With help from less semiotics more psychedelics

Joe and Bob McClure

McClure's Pickles

Detroit, USA (2007)

Brothers Joe and Bob McClure started their company, McClure's Pickles, in 2006 with their great-grandmother Lala's pickle recipe. Having practiced the art of pickle-making for years under the tutelage of their father, mother, and grandfather, they turned the family talent for pickling into a successful business using the freshest, most local produce they can get their hands on. They just might be the most diversified picklers in history; Joe is completing a doctoral degree in physiology and is also a classical musician, while Bob is an actor and comedy writer.

Photo: John Urbanek

Muotohiomo
Noa Bembibre, Rasmus Snabb,
Aleksi Perälä, Aki Suvanto, Saku Sysiö

SIS. Deli+Café
Helsinki, Finland (2008)

SIS. Deli+Café was launched in 2008 by two
sisters, Anu Syrmä and Kaisa Leikola, who left
their corporate jobs to fulfill a dream of building something of their own that they truly
believed in. Their products can be enjoyed with
a good conscience; everything is carefully chosen
from high-quality producers in Finland and
abroad, the majority of which are organically or
locally produced. The deli offers fresh food prepared daily from their own recipes and a range
of prepackaged products including black currant
leaf drink, blueberry licorice, sea buckthorn
marmalade, and dried winter chanterelles.
The look and feel of the product range, Goodness
from Finland, was designed together with the
design agency Muotohiomo. The stores have an
atmosphere that is modern, yet cosy, while the
prepackaged items allow easy takeaway.

Client: Anu Syrmä, Kaisa Leikola
Photo: Sami Repo

· 40 ·

Zita Majoros, Claudia Martins, Tibor Varady

Printa Café
Budapest, Hungary (2009)

Printa Café, owned by Zita Majoros, Claudia Martins, and Tibor Varady, and located in downtown Budapest, maintains a high standard of quality by employing professional baristas and serving espresso from the acclaimed The Coffee Collective roastery made with a La Marzocco machine. It is the only coffee shop in Budapest serving filtered coffee brewed by the cup using the syphon, French press, and pour over methods. All coffee is sourced in the Direct Trade system, which ensures a high price for the farmer and exceptional quality for the consumer. The space is also a design shop and gallery.

Photo: Szeicz Anita

Martin Schmöller,
Michael Spindler

Pommes Boutique
Munich, Germany (2006)

Munich's Pommes Boutique pairs unique interior
design by architect Martin Schmöller and designer
Michael Spindler with delicious food including
original Belgian fries and 20 dips. Traditional organic
sausages, couscous-lamb-burgers, prawn skewers,
and goat cheese with a sesame nut crust are served as
side dishes, while homemade lemonades and desserts
round out the beverage and dessert categories.

Mind Design

Le Pain Quotidien identity
London, UK (2008, 2009)

Mind Design created a number of packaging and promotional materials for the international bakery Le Pain Quotidien. Illustrations by Aude van Ryn tie the various pieces together including a screen-printed takeaway pique-nique box, which is also used for display purposes in all UK shops, packaging for a range of teas sold in the various Le Pain Quotidien stores (whose illustrations refer to different types of kettles used for brewing tea), table cards to promote the teas, and a screen-printed cotton bread bag.

Client: Le Pain Quotidien
Illustration: Aude van Ryn

Williams Murray Hamm

Yes Please Organic Soups
Berlin, Germany (2007)

Yes Please Foods is a German company specializing in pre-made meals that use high quality ingredients without the addition of additives or preservatives. Yes Please soups are packaged using a sturdy, resealable container with a label designed by Williams Murray Hamm that incorporates an illustration by Berlin-based illustrator Martin Haacke.

Client: Yes Please Foods GmbH
Photo: Melissa Hostetler

Cornwell Design

Capital Kitchen

Melbourne, Australia (2009)

Melbourne caterers, The Big Group, created
Capital Kitchen as a new retail home wares
and food concept store to complement the new
luxury wing of Chadstone Shopping Centre.
Cornwell Design positioned the brand to repre-
sent the style and tone of the modern farmhouse;
the illustrations mix a variety of nostalgic food
items such as the classic 1960s milk bottle, egg
cups, and preserve jars. Representing a time in
history when things were slower, quieter, and
less chaotic, the experience provides customers
with a break from their busy city lives, trans-
porting them to the warm comfort of a country
farmhouse.

Client: The Big Group

Mind Design

Tea
London, UK (2007)

Mind Design created the identity and overall design concept for a London tea shop, Tea, whose first shop is located next to the popular tourist destination of Saint Paul's Cathedral. In response to the resurgence in popularity of tea, the concept aimed to use a color scheme to categorize similar types of teas. In doing so, the complex world of tea is made more accessible to newcomers. The logo uses the inner part of the letter 'a' to form a tea leaf — which is then changed in color according to the type of tea it represents. This identity has been applied to packaging, menus, and interior graphics and is occasionally contrasted with references to old-fashioned English tea culture such as tea cozies and doilies.

Client: Tea Limited

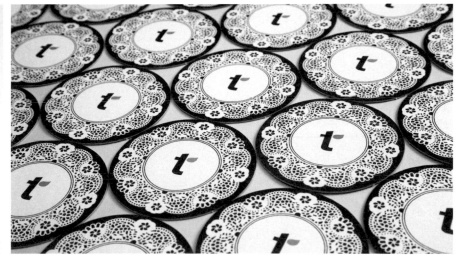

Couple

Zann Wan, Kelvin Lok

brill.
Singapore (2008)

brill is a food take-out business that occupies small storefront spaces in dense urban settings where consumers want to be amused and dazzled while receiving care and attention. Design firm Couple melded precision with frivolity in the branding; the logo has a ring of varied border designs beginning with an outer scalloped border that moves inward to Greek fret motifs, checkers, and a cross-stitch pattern.

Client: Simply Bread

ninkipen!
Yasuo Imazu

panscape 2jo
Osaka, Japan (2010)

ninkipen! designed this minimalist remodel of an existing space for the Japanese bakery panscape. Bread is showcased in a vintage glass box on top of a 1000 pound log, while concrete is the material of choice for the counter, shelves, and floors. The wood-burning oven is the first thing one sees upon walking through the door; the glowing mouse hole (what bakery would be authentic without one?) takes a moment to locate.

Client: Tetsuya Kubo
Photo: Hiroki Kawata

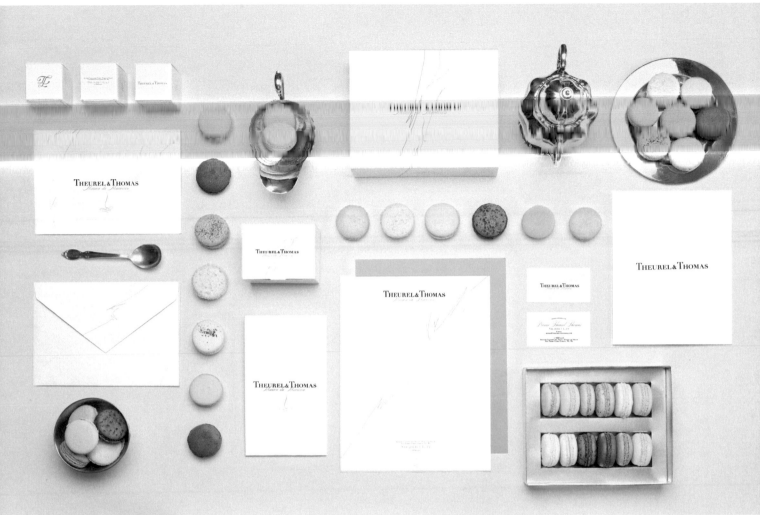

Anagrama

Theurel & Thomas
San Pedro Garza García, Mexico (2009)

Theurel & Thomas is the first patisserie in
Mexico to specialize in French macaroons.
The brand bases its business on retail sales, making the design and ambience of the stores a key
focus. Taking this into consideration, Anagrama
created an imposing brand that emphasizes
the unique value, elegance, and detail of this delicate dessert. Located in one of Latin America's
most affluent suburbs, the Theurel & Thomas patisserie space radiates an air of exclusivity, using
white as the primary color to focus all attention
on its colorful macaroons. The cyan and magenta
lines of the identity inject a vanguard vision
while the Didot typeface presents the brand with
sophistication. Details were an essential part of
this project, making the value of the brand and
the exclusivity of the product stand out.

Credits: in collaboration with Germán Dehesa and
Roberto Treviño

Anagrama

Theurel & Thomas
San Pedro Garza García, Mexico (2009)

Whimsy & Spice
Mark Sopchak, Jenna Park

Mark Sopchak and Jenna Park have a combined background in the culinary arts and graphic design. They started Whimsy & Spice in 2008.

Top
Homemade Marshmallows
Brooklyn, USA (2008)

The soft texture and airy structure of homemade marshmallows make them a perfect accompaniment to hot cocoa or coffee.

Left
Pumpkin Ginger Sandwich Cookies
Brooklyn, USA (2008)

A creamy white chocolate filling, delicately spiked with white pepper, is sandwiched between two spiced pumpkin ginger cookies and dusted with sparkling sugar.

Above
Marshmallow Party Favors
Brooklyn, USA (2008)

Caramel marshmallow favors with a custom label were created for a baby shower.

Photo: All images by Jenna Park

33 Coffees
Dave Selden

33 Cups of Coffee/33 Coffees
Portland, USA (2010)

33 Coffees is a coffee journal that provides an easy way to record coffee tasting notes in a notebook small enough to fit in your pocket. Designed for coffee novices and pros alike, 33 Coffees can be used in many ways because the pages are flexible and easy to use: just check some boxes and enter a few basic facts to record and remember multiple brew methods, varietals, and roast profiles.

Client: 33 Books Co.
Photo: Dave Selden
Additional credits: Latte poured by Amber, barista at Coava Coffee in Portland, Oregon

Caitlin Williams Freeman

Blue Bottle Art Cakes
San Francisco, USA (2010)

Caitlin Williams Freeman is the pastry chef for the San Francisco Museum of Modern Art's Blue Bottle Coffee Bar. Her work involves making sweets inspired by the museum's art collection, including pieces by Richard Diebenkorn, Piet Mondrian, Richard Serra, and Olafur Eliasson. She translates these iconic works into cakes, cookies, drinks, and ice cream, allowing museum visitors a fresh way to enjoy the what they have seen.

Client: SFMOMA Blue Bottle Coffee Bar
Photo: Charles Villyard

Amseldrossel Design Studio

Ina Liesefeld, Alexander H. Weber

Yoli Berlin

Berlin, Germany (2009)

Yoli offers pure white frozen yogurt together with fresh fruit. Amseldrossel Design Studio used large windows and an open space plan to create a relaxing atmosphere that is sufficiently lit with ample amounts of natural light. On this white backdrop, colorful layered shapes mimic the colorful toppings of the yogurt. The counter is positioned in the middle of the room and is open on both sides so that customers can see the preparation of their customized frozen yogurt.

Client: Young Jun, Yoli Frozen Yogurt
Photo: Jon Hoekstra, www.jonadriehoekstra.com

Chocolate Company
Kerkrade, Netherlands (2004)

Thinking there must be another way to make homemade hot chocolate in a single serving without all the mess, the Chocolate Company set out to invent a way and came up with the Hotchocspoon, a chunky piece of chocolate that is stirred into hot milk.

Coolhaus
Natasha Case and Freya Estreller

Coolhaus Ice Cream Sandwiches
Los Angeles, USA (2009)

Natasha Case and Freya Estreller began selling their architecturally inspired ice cream sandwiches from a postal truck bought on Craigslist. The sandwiches, with names like Mintimalism and Mies Vanilla Rohe, are handmade using sustainably produced dairy products and local ingredients. Each sandwich is wrapped in a customizable, edible wrapper that is all-natural and calorie-free and can be printed on with edible ink.

Photo: Brian Leatart; Truck photo by Stephanie Diani

Designliga

Das Neue Kubitscheck
Munich, Germany (2010)

Armin Stegbauer is many things: a punk,
a Greenpeace activist, and a cafe owner. His goal
is to free cakes and gateaux from their years of
imprisonment behind the bars of the crocheted
doilies, cologne, and dusty Sunday traditions of
Germany. Stegbauer is savior of the Cafe Kubitscheck in Munich, a traditional confectioner from
the 1950s. Along with design firm Designliga,
he revamped the confectioner's tradition for the
modern age— but not without preserving some
of the endearing aspects of Germany's confec-
tionery culture.

Client: Armin Stegbauer

Designliga

Das Neue Kubitscheck, coporate identity
Munich, Germany (2010)

The project included packaging design, corporate identity, and interior design. The saying, "Tell me what music you listen to, and I'll tell you who you are" served as a blueprint for the look and feel of the campaign and for the subsequent implementation of Das Neue Kubitscheck (The New Kubitscheck). The corporate design is multifaceted, dynamic, and free of rigid frameworks; it needed to be vibrant and in a permanent state of flux, able to adapt to developments instead of compelling alignment. The statement "Fuck the Backmischung," (Fuck the Cake Mix) is Stegbauer's mission statement. It expresses the uncompromising quality standards he applies to his products and is the journal, menu, and mouthpiece of the movement.

Client: Armin Stegbauer
Photo: Pascale Gambarte (cafe front view),
Designliga (packaging)

ESRAWE and CADENA+ASOC
Ignacio Cadena, Héctor Esrawe

Cielito Querido Cafe
Mexico (2010)

Esrawe and Cadena + Asoc drew their inspiration for the design of the Cielito Querido Cafe from the the games, colors, symbolic language, and illustrations of the late nineteenth and early twentieth centuries. Latin American signs and product labels from old grocery stores speak a graphic language representative of a culture that is rich in history, but always open to reinvention. The cafe's name references the playful spirit of language in Latin America and its design rescues the aesthetics of popular Latin-American culture by reinventing it in a neo-retro style that fuses graphics from French and Spanish colonial times with modern Latin American media. These elements are subtly integrated and produce a contemporary product that is appealing to both a Latin and a universal audience.

Client: Grupo ADO
Photo: Jaime Navarro
Additional credits: Branding by CADENA+ASOC/Ignacio Cadena, Collaborators: Nora Cavazos Luna, Rocío Serna González; Interiors by ESRAWE studio Hector Esrawe, Project Management by Joaquín Cevallos, Coordination by Arq. senior Arturo Gasca, Collaborators: Sara Casillas, Ian Castillo, Jennifer Sacal, Roberto Escalante, Didier López, Irvin Martínez, Cynthia Cárdenas, Jorge Bracho DMG; Architects: Miguel de la Torre, Marco Antonio Espinoza, Adolfo Pérez

ESRAWE and CADENA+ASOC

Ignacio Cadena, Héctor Esrawe

Cielito Querido Cafe

Mexico (2010)

The Metrics
Elle Kunnos de Voss

What Happens When
New York, USA (2011)

The Metrics designed What Happens When, a temporary restaurant installation that transforms itself every 30 days. It will live for nine months in a reclaimed space in New York City, changing the space, the food, and the soundscape every month in order to explore what a dining experience can be — and how the traditional expectations of dining out can be played with.

Client: John Fraser (Chef)
Photo: Felix de Voss

Chocolate Pie Chart.

By Mary & Matt.

Net weight: 5.5oz (156g)

Mary & Matt

Mary Matson, Matt Even

CHOCOLATE EDITIONS

Chocolate Pie Chart

Opposite page,
top to bottom, left to right

Neapolitan Bar
Black and White Bar
Standard Bar Packaging
Eat Me Bar (milk)
Primary Packaging
Primary Salted Dark Bar
Primary Strawberry Bar
Primary Milk Bar
New York, USA (2009)

Mary & Matt make chocolate bars in small
batches with high quality ingredients. Each batch
draws its theme from pop culture and everyday
objects, which are re-imagined into chocolate bars.

Photo: Mary & Matt.

Chocolate Editions.

Net weight: 3oz (85g)

EAT ME

Mary & Matt.

EAT ME

Chocolate Editions.

Bernotat & Co Design Studio
Anke Bernotat

100 Gram Tangram
Amsterdam, Netherlands (2010)

100 Gram Tangram combines a 1000 year old Chinese puzzle with a chocolate bar — and the question as to why chocolate bars always have to be broken in a boring grid of squares. 100 Gram Tangram is a chocolate version of the Chinese dissection puzzle; break the chocolate apart and you end up with seven geometric shapes that can be put together to form figures. The aim is to recreate a specific shape — in this case a person, an animal, or an object of desire. With roughly 6000 possible Tangram configurations, 100 Gram Tangram offers hours of fun. To manufacture the Tangram chocolate, Anke Bernotat teamed up with small German chocolatier Sächsische Schokoladenmanufaktur, one of a few who still produce artisanal chocolates.

Client: Sächsische Schokoladenmanufaktur
Photo: Rogier Chang

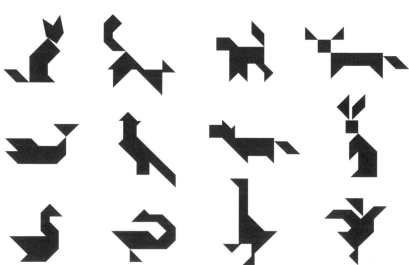

Fine & Raw Chocolate

Raw Cacao Series
Brooklyn, USA (2009)

Fine & Raw is a collaboration of chocolatiers, artists, photographers, painters, chefs, ice cream makers, candy makers, friends, music, tea drinkers, farmers, dancers, philosophers, travelers, angels, and aliens who handcraft their confections in Brooklyn, New York. The concept is to make authentic and organic food while keeping a sense of epicurean chocolate. The packaging is recycled textured kraft paper and the designs are inspired by minimal aesthetics and the world of edible botany.

Photo: Kelly Hoffman

Raw Cacao Series

Photo: Seze Devres

Cacao & Agave Bonbons

Photo: Seze Devres

Designers and Farmers

Skyrkonfekt

Reykjavík and Erpstaðir, Iceland (2011)

Rjómabúíð Erpsstaðir is a family company that values honesty and transparency in their production process. The farm's cows live in the best possible conditions and are free to go where they like. Under the same roof, the farmers produce their artisan dairy products with affection.
The Skyrkonfekt is custom-made by The Designers and Farmers Project for The Dairy Farm Erpsstaði. It is a quality treat, coated with Valrhona chocolate and filled with homemade Skyr from Erpsstaði. The Skyrkonfekt is produced at the Erpsstaði farm and was officially launched during DesignMarch in Reykjavík, 2011.

Client: The Dairy Farm Erpsstaðir
Initiator: Iceland Academy of the Arts
Photo: Vigfús Birgisson
Additional credits: Sigríður Sigurjónsdóttir (Professor of Product Design at The Iceland Academy of the Arts), Guðfinna Mjöll Magnúsdóttir and Brynhildur Pálsdóttir (design directors), Jordi Serra (graphic designer), Kristín Birna Bjarnadóttir and Sabrina Stiegler (product designers), Örvar Birgisson (the conditori chef, the food scientists at Matís, a research center for the food industry), and the farmers Þorgrímur Einar Guðbjartsson and Helga Guðmundsdóttir, along with their partner Ingvar Bæringsson, dairy expert.

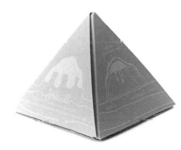

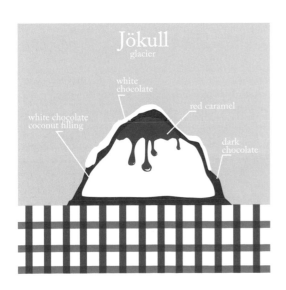

Borðið
Brynhildur Pálsdóttir

Chocolate Mountains
Reykjavík, Iceland (2007)

Jökull glaciers are one of Iceland's most spectacular sights and have forcefully shaped many of the country's fjords and valleys. Borðið's Chocolate Mountains reproduce Iceland's glaciers in miniature.

Marc Trotereau, Elisa Valenzuela

Croquillages
France (2011)

This salted cocktail snack is made with frozen seashells that contain their "fruit" and uncooked cake dough. When the seashells are placed in the oven, the cake dough rises, turning the shell into a mold.

Photo: Marc Trotereau

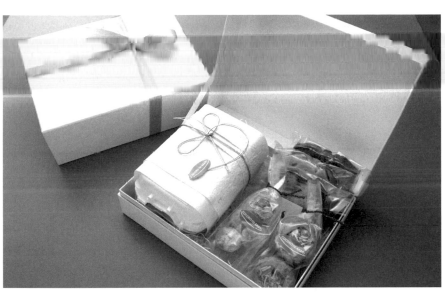

COCORO no AKARI
Project Team

CHOCO TAMAGO & TAMAGO
Pudding
Tokyo, Japan (2007)

Eggshells were reused as a pudding mold and for presentation of the product.

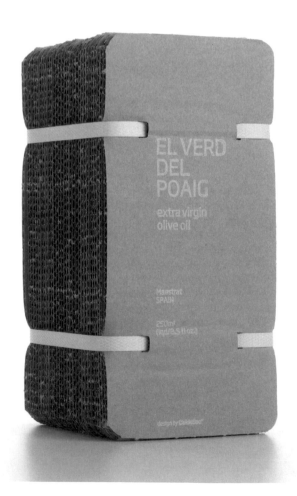

CuldeSac

El Verd del Poaig
Valencia, Spain (2010)

Following the success of El Mil del Poaig— designated by the media as "the world's most expensive olive oil"— El Poaig presents El Verd del Poaig, a unique extra virgin olive oil taken from the olive trees of El Maestrat on the Mediterranean coast of Spain. The packaging, designed by CuldeSac™, is a slender bottle of white, bisque-glazed ceramic that contrasts with a protective thermo-sealed cardboard laminate structure. By pulling away the cardboard petals of the packaging, a new version of El Poaig reveals itself to be a perfect match between accessible luxury and sustainability.

Client: El Poaig

Couple

Zann Wan, Kelvin Lok

Simply Sandwich Delivery Box
Singapore (2007)

Singapore's Simply Sandwich bakes up fresh rolls filled with a variety of tasty fillings. For the launch of the delivery side of the business, Couple designed a stackable box, strong enough to cart freshly filled rolls around town to waiting customers — and flexible enough to transform into a tray once the lid is zip-ripped. Each box is fastened with a sleeve of 47 kiss-cut stickers printed with contact information, products, lunch invitations, and hidden messages that promote the shop and its delivery business.

Client: Simply Bread

THE SKY IS THE LIMIT

Keeping things simple doesn't mean keeping things bland. In fact, it means the opposite in the mobile and open air food business. These entrepreneurs take their time to craft unusual interpretations of well-known standards and experiment with new ideas. Making the most of small, mobile work spaces means focusing on quality and being sustainable and efficient. Whether located in front of a Manhattan office building or parked on the beach in L.A., mobile food is as much about bringing the food to the consumer as it is about taking the customer on a journey to new places and experiences.

Der Kaffeefreund
Dominik Schweer

Der Kaffeefreund —
Munster's First Bike Cafe
Munster, Germany (2010)

A utility bike has Dutch origins but it was modified to be an espresso bike by Paul Sabin in the UK. The bike has three wheels with a canopy over the working area and is outfitted with a gas-powered espresso machine. Der Kaffeefreund has catered events in cities all over Germany, but makes its permanent home in south Munster in front of St. Joseph's from Sunday through Thursday.

Photo: Yavuz Arslan, © NRW.BANK / YavuzArslan. com (large photo); Stefanie König (Small photo)
Additional credits: Modification of the Dutch utility bike by Paul Sabin

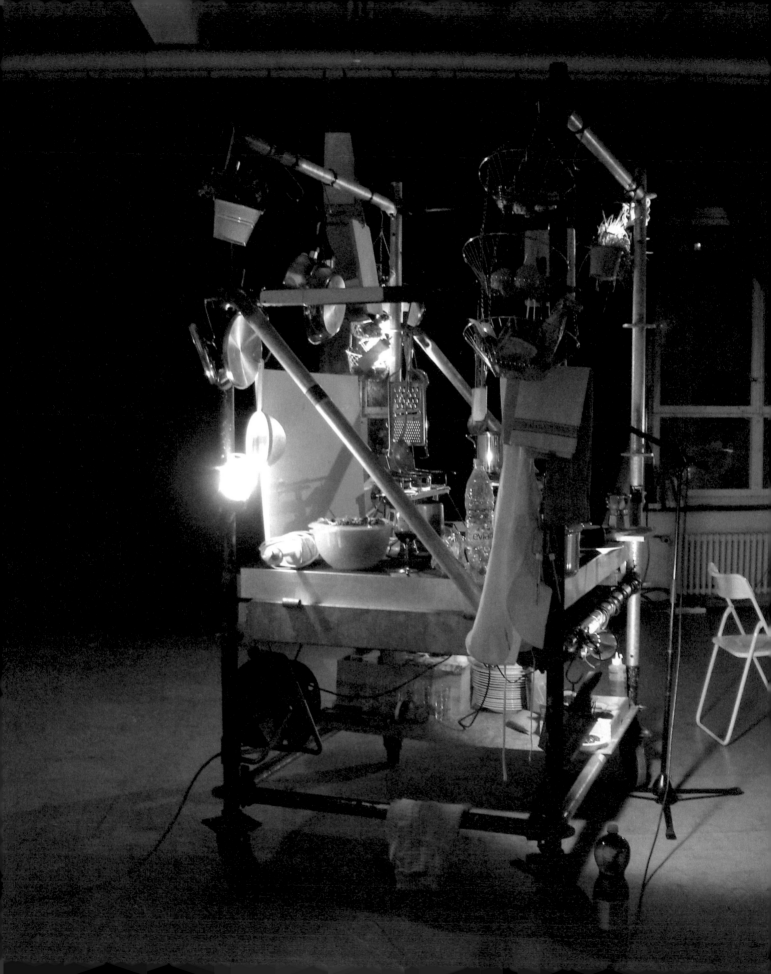

Kueng Caputo

Sarah Kueng & Lovis Caputo

Improkitchen
Zurich, Switzerland (2008)

Eva Maria Küpfer and Stefanie Grubenmann are
choreographers and dancers who also curate dinners.
Kueng Caputo created the Improkitchen as the base
for their improvisational process and cooking. For
the opening ceremony of Zurich's theatrical season,
the Improkitchen was rolled through the city with
a chef preparing food inside of it. Upon arrival at the
Rote Fabrik, the finished meal was served. In addition
to its role as a functional kitchen, the Improkitchen
was also a stage. Performances continued for one year
at the Fabriktheater Zurich.

Client: Eva Maria Küpfer, Stefanie Grubenmann
Photo: Christian Glaus (outdoor), Barbara Schlittler (indoor)

BLUE MARBLE ICE CREAM
Blue Marble Dreams
Jennie Dundas, Alexis Miesen

Inzozi Nziza (Sweet Dreams)
Butare, Rwanda (2010)

Blue Marble Dreams is the nonprofit initiative of Blue Marble Ice Cream whose mission is to support communities in need through the unlikely medium of ice cream. Blue Marble Dreams partnered with a group of women in Butare, Rwanda, to create Rwanda's first local ice cream shop. Inzozi Nziza (Sweet Dreams) provides training and employment to local women and a welcoming place where everyone can relax and indulge. The shop offers soft serve ice cream produced with local dairy, sugar, and fruit. It also roasts and sells Rwandan coffee, in-house. Inzozi Inziza's workers are shareholders with an active, invested role in the business. In addition to extensive training in shop operations and general business practices, they attend English and computer classes.

Photo: Piper Watson
Additional credits: Jennie Dundas, Alexis Miesen in collaboration with their partners in Rwanda and project manager Nikki Grey

People's Pops
New York, USA (2010)

People's Pops takes local fresh fruit and turns it into ice pops and shaved ice, selling them at various New York City locations and delivering them to office parties, backyard BBQs, corporate events, weddings, and annulments.

Kogi BBQ

Los Angeles and Orange County, USA (2010)

Cruising the streets of Los Angeles and Orange County, Kogi BBQ's color-coded taco trucks (named Azul, Verde, Roja, Naranja, and Rosita) serve up Korean-Mexican food including kimchi quesadillas, spicy pork tacos— and a Pacman burger.

Photo: Abby C. Abanes, Lataco.com

Samira Mahboubian, Grant Di Mille

Sweetery NYC
New York, USA (2009)

It was the financial crisis that made Samira Mahboubian and Grant Di Mille consider opening a mobile food business. They designed and built everything for the cafe themselves, including buying the truck on Craigslist and branding the business. Since June of 2010, the event and promotion side of the Sweetery has seen a steep rise in demand; they have produced major projects for corporations such as American Express, *Food Network Magazine*, Saks Fifth Avenue, and *Real Simple* magazine.

Oleg Voss

Schnitzel & Things
New York, USA (2009)

In 2009, Schnitzel fan Oleg Voss started serving schnitzel to hungry New Yorkers from his Schnitzel & Things food truck. The hand-pounded cutlets and fresh ingredients became so popular that he opened a restaurant in 2011.

Donny Tsang

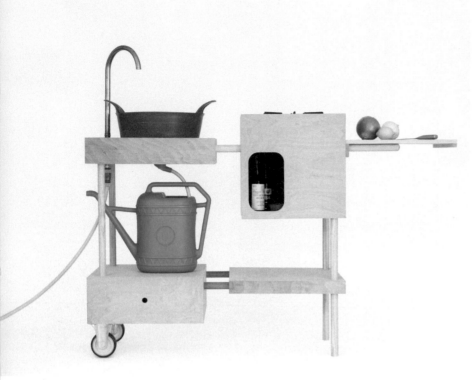

Studiomama
Nina Tolstrup

Outdoor Kitchen
London, UK (2010)

Studiomama's _Outdoor Kitchen_ has a gas bottle-powered cooktop, a sink, a chopping board, and storage for crockery and utensils. Waste water, which is collected by a watering can underneath the sink, can be used for watering plants. The product instructions give different options for construction depending on the user's level of carpentry skill. All the components are easily sourced from hardware stores and the materials needed to construct the rest come from one sheet of plywood, several broomsticks, and some screws. Surface treatment can be tailored to suit personal preference and taste (the version pictured is treated with Osmo Oil).

Photo: Studiomama

Andaz Hotel, Christmas Trolley, Liverpool Street, London
London, UK (2010)

Andaz Hotel commissioned designer Nina Tolstrup of Studiomama to create a sensory winterscape in the main entrance of the hotel from December 6–31. Replete with preparation areas, cooktop, and oven, Tolstrup's mobile Christmas cart not only served freshly baked cookies, mince pies, and warming drinks throughout the day, it also filled the hotel with abundant Christmas aromas and became a spot for guests and visitors to gather and share the festive spirit.

Photo: Nina Tolstrup

Daniel Unterberg,
Isabell Weiland

Stadtküche
Berlin, Germany (2009)

Daniel Unterberg and Isabell Weiland built the
Stadtküche for the cultural festival 48h Neu-
kölln. The kitchen in a bike trailer is mobile,
self-sufficient, and offers (in addition to cooking
essentials) a long eating table, at which passersby
may take a seat. The inside of the trailer accom-
modates tableware, pots and pans, and two water
containers. The cooking module consists of a
counter with a wash basin, cutting board, spice
rack, and four burners. Attached are two equally
long tables that can be connected during trans-
port to create storage for ten stools. An umbrella
over the kitchen module allows the chef to cook
comfortably for long periods of time.

Photo: Nicole Erbe, Rolf Eusterschulte

Attridge & Cole
Sam Alexander

Belfast, Northern Ireland (2010)

Attridge & Cole can be found serving hand crafted coffees and pastries from their classic French commercial vehicle, a lovingly-restored Citroen H Van. Totally self-contained and completely mobile, their coffee and pastries can be served in any location.

Design and branding: Hurson (www.hurson.ie)

Photo: www.oppositepage.com

ATTRIDGE & COLE™

COFFEE CO.

KUBIDEH
KITCHEN

Conflict Kitchen USA
Jon Rubin, Dawn Weleski

Conflict Kitchen
Pittsburgh, USA (2010)

Conflict Kitchen serves cuisine from countries
that the United States is in conflict with.
The restaurant's menu and storefront identity
rotate every four months and are augmented by
events, performances, and discussions. The second iteration of Conflict Kitchen was presented
via Bolani Pazi, an Afghan restaurant serving a
savory homemade Afghan turnover. Developed
in collaboration with members of the Afghan
community, the bolani was packaged in a custom
wrapper and contained interviews with Afghans.
Conflict Kitchen creates a platform for first-per-
son discussion of international conflict, culture,
and politics while introducing a rotating venue
for culinary and cultural diversity in Pittsburgh.
Future iterations will focus on countries such as
North Korea and Venezuela.

Photo: Conflict Kitchen

PostlerFerguson

Nouveau Neolithic
London, UK (2007)

Nouveau Neolithic by PostlerFerguson is a range of tools for post-apocalyptic gourmands. By replacing electrical power with collective labor, small groups of people can produce refined gourmet cuisine from simple staples and foraged foods. Nouveau Neolithic draws inspiration from communal cooking practices that emerged during the Depression and the World Wars in America and Europe and proposes a new take on sustainability by focussing on transforming the limitations imposed by global warming and resource depletion into positive new social practices.

COMMUNITY
GARDEN
EDUCATIONAL
WORKSHOP

1

3

Archeworks
Rachel Belanger, Maria Kulesa, Derek Layes,
Catherine Muller, Adam Panza, Mason Pritchett,
Geoffrey Salvatore, Jesse Vogler

Mobile Food Collective
Chicago, USA (2010)

In response to growing public interest and
awareness of the social, economic, and health
benefits associated with local food production,
Archeworks developed a mobile architecture to
engage communities across Chicago in a new
food culture through collaborative exchange and
education. The MFC is many things: an education and exchange platform for planting, growing,
and cooking; demonstrations and distribution of
seeds, soil, compost, and produce; a space activa-
tor within a community event; or the centerpiece
of a harvest dinner. Its campaign— to develop
and strengthen a system of cultural infrastructure
that incorporates the themes of heritage, owner-
ship, exchange, and connection— inspires people
to play a more active role in the food cycle.
Archeworks advances design in the public interest
and inspires collaborative action to shape more
ecologically sustainable cities. Their major objec-
tive is for the design professions to have greater
influence on community development, environmental health, and urban policy.

Photo: Mason Pritchett

2

ON design
Osamu Nishida, Hiroaki Harasaki

Roppongi Nouen FARM
Roppongi, Tokyo, Japan (2010)

The Roppongi Nouen FARM is an urban farm located in the center of Tokyo. ON design built an iron structure that supports houses of glass and echos the forms of the cityscape that rise around it. The resulting transparency allows visitors to see how vegetables are grown — and then eat the vegetables at the restaurant next door to the farm. As a farm that has been transported from the countryside into the city, it is a place where agriculture and people can become close.

Photo: Koichi Torimura

ON design
Osamu Nishida, Ken Shikauchi, Hiroaki Harasaki

Roppongi Nouen
Roppongi, Tokyo, Japan (2009)

Roppongi Nouen is a restaurant doubling as an agricultural experiment, operated by the sons and daughters of a farmer. Their idea, to connect rural farms and urban cities, began with using soil to renovate a former French restaurant. Soil was chosen as a material because of its importance to farmers. Farms across Japan supplied the soil, which was applied to the walls during a workshop led by the master plasterer Naoki Kusumi.

Photo: Koichi Torimura

Nomadisch Grün

Prinzessinnengärten
Berlin, Germany (2009)

The Prinzessinengärten is an organic community garden focusing on education and public relations in the areas of environmental conservation, biodiversity, and sustainable urban development. In order to also be economically sustainable, they are committed to creating a financially functioning foundation. To achieve this, they are commercially active, directly marketing the vegetables from their kitchen garden and recruiting active donors for their education, youth, and environmental projects. Support from engaged volunteers and businesses who feel strong social and ecological responsibilities are also an important part of the business. In the Thousand Green program, for example, participants can be direct supporters when they sponsor of one of the garden's vegetable patches.

Photo: All images by Marco Clausen / Prinzessinnengärten

Nomadisch Grün

Prinzessinnenagärten
Berlin, Germany (2009)

Maaike Bertens

Public Pie
Netherlands and traveling through Europe (2008)

Public Pie is a mobile pie bakery whose aim is
to bring a lively and intimate atmosphere to public places. The open kitchen designed by Maaike
Bertens demonstrates the baking process to
the public while a bench situated above the kitch-
en lets people warm up while enjoying a piece of
pie. First created for an exhibition initiated and
produced by the carpenter and artist Piet Bergman,
the project grew into a successful business and has
since received invitations to participate in cultural
openings, events, and festivals such as Ventura
Lambrate during the Milan Furniture Fair.

Additional credits: Furniture built by Piet Bergman

Maaike Bertens

Public Pie

Photo: Claudia Castaldi

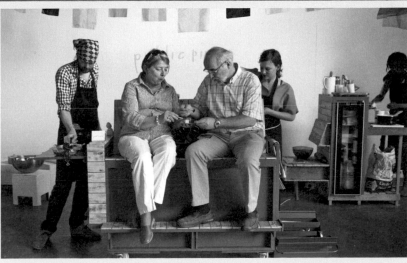

PlayLab
Archie Lee Coates IV, Jeffrey Franklin, Brian W. Jones, Haik Avanian, and Breane Kostyk

PieLab
Greensboro, USA (2009)

PieLab is a pie shop with a simple mission: encouraging conversation over a great slice of pie. Located in Greensboro, a divided southern town in rural Alabama, it was created as a neutral place for the community to share inspirational stories and ideas that could improve the town. PieLab also hosts community outreach events and encourages locals to collaborate with PieLab designers to create what they want to see in Greensboro. Located in a donated building and built from reclaimed building materials and thrift store finds, the original pop-up pie shop cost almost nothing to produce. With the help of design firm PlayLab, PieLab has relocated down the street to a newly expanded storefront that is equipped with space for community gatherings and events.

Client: Project M
Photo: PlayLab and Brian W. Jones
Additional credits: In collaboration with Project M and HERO

Edible Tales
Frankie Unsworth, Rachel Khoo

The transitory culinary project Edible Tales was founded by Rachel Khoo and Frankie Unsworth in early 2010. Its first chapter, Edible Immigration Tales, was held over the course of three nights in Sydney, Australia. Four months later, Edible Tapestry Tales was held at Victoria's State of Design Festival during the Australian Tapestry Workshop. Inspired by the workshop's looms and colorful tapestries, Rachel and Frankie conceived a menu and table-setting that reflected the colors, textures, techniques, and history of tapestry making, including woven fruit and

clothed scarlet dashi with Gobelins boulettes (the Gobelins were a family of French dyers who discovered the secret of dying the color scarlet). In 2011, Edible Tales came to Buenos Aires, Argentina, for a book-themed dinner hosted on a rooftop that explored the history of books and paper through a four-course menu in which diners were asked to become creative with their food; edible paper made from a crispy flatbread was served with a paintbrush and three edible paints nestled in an artist's palette.

Edible Tales Buenos Aires
Buenos Aires, Argentina (February 2011)

Photo: All images by Caitlin M. Kelly

Papyrus Paper with Edible inks
Buenos Aires, Argentina (February 2011)

Edible Tales Buenos Aires
Buenos Aires, Argentina (2011)

Droog, Marije Vogelzang,
Hansje van Halem,
and sloom.org

Go Slow Café
New York, USA (2009)

The Go Slow Café is a project by Droog with
Marije Vogelzang, sloom.org (Rianne Makkink,
Herman Verkerk), and Hansje van Halem.
Conceived as a traveling cafe where slow food is
served by elderly local volunteers, the Go Slow
Café aims to make guests feel like they are visit-
ing a private home while drawing awareness to
where their food comes from and how they are
experiencing it. Its location on Governors Island
during the Dutch design festival Pioneers of
Change removed it slightly from Manhattan—
a perfect location for reflecting the cafe's com-
mitment to slowing down.

Client: Pioneers of Change
Photo: Isauro Cairo

Brooklyn Slate Company

Slate Coasters
Brooklyn, USA (2011)

The pieces of slate sold by the Brooklyn Slate Company — which can be used for food presentation, coasters, and trivets — are hand-picked from co-owner Kristy Hadeka's family slate quarry in upstate New York. She and partner Sean Tice, a graphic designer, refine the pieces at their Brooklyn studio by giving the edges a uniformly rugged finish and the overall surface a food-safe cleaning. Committed to reusable products, the Brooklyn Slate Company has designed their packaging out of elements that may easily be repurposed.

Photo: Michael Harlan Turkell, harlanturk.com

Malin Elmlid

Bread Exchange
Berlin, Germany (since 2010)

When Malin Elmlid stopped eating white bread in 2009, she decided to start baking sour-dough bread. After a year of practice, she was skilled enough to take an internship with Swe-den's premier sourdough baker, Manfred Enock-son. Back home in Berlin, she found that family, friends, and neighbors could not eat all of her sourdough overstock. And so the Bread Exchange was born; instead of selling the bread, she traded it with others who had something unique to give. Her bread has brought her marmalade, herbs, backyard eggs, photography services, vanilla from Madagascar, Austrian wine, and about 900 friends from around the world. Her sourdough starters have travelled around the world with her — one was even made during a riding holiday in the Sinai Desert. Why trade and not sell? Each loaf takes at least 24 hours to make and is folded every 20 minutes during the first hours. Not everything is for sale.

FOODZINES

A story about food is a good story to tell. Passionate foodies—amateurs and professionals alike—have developed a number of new formats for reading and writing about food. In addition to food blogs, independent food magazines offer what traditional commercial magazines cannot; the personal involvement of their creators and a willingness to take chances when it comes to approaching the broad topic of food. Instead of working with commercial photographers and journalists, independent magazines are more likely to collaborate with artists, allowing them the freedom to interpret a given theme. This approach results in publications whose form and content reflect the values of craftsmanship, beauty, and sustainability that their publishers bring to the topic of food.

How to

MAKE BOUILLA- BAISSE

BY
ANDREW TARLOW
&
KATE HULING

**Andrew Tarlow, Anna Dunn,
August Heffner**

Diner Journal
Brooklyn, USA (Since 2006)

DINER JOURNAL

FALL 2000   NO. 16   THE HOW TO ISSUE

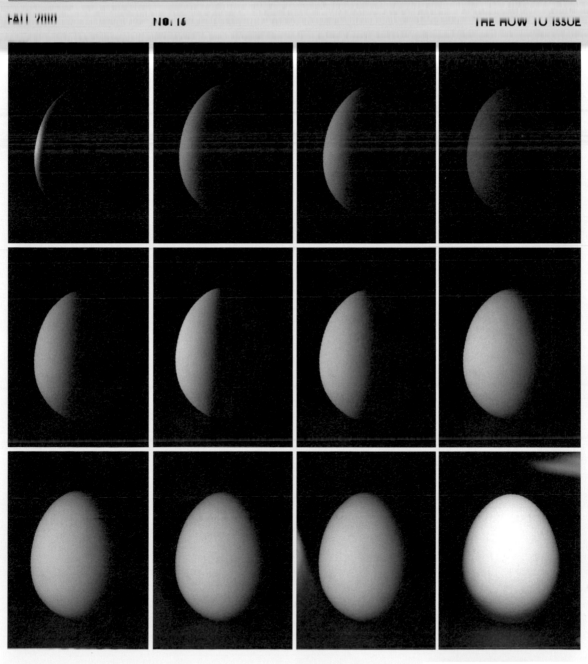

$9   NO ADS

HOW TO HUNT
A SNAPPING TURTLE

BY MARK FIRTH
ILLUSTRATION BY JULIET JACOBSON

FOR THREE WEEKS after the birth of our eleven ducklings the mother and father proudly led them around the pond, ducking and diving for tasty morsels and splashing around like they had never heard of cassoulet. They all slept under a tree next to the pond and every visitor refuted the serendipity of our perfect homestead, pigs in the pig pen, chickens in the coop and ducks on the pond.

Then one night at 3am we heard a tremendous quacking. I jumped up and running naked through the kitchen grabbed the cleaver. Bettina was right behind me with a flash light, and after all the feathers had settled down, two of the ducks were missing and the rest were huddled frightened in the middle of the pond. We checked the nest, no sign of any intruders, and mildly traumatized we went to bed. The next morning we found one of the babies. It had two teeth holes in its neck and the blood had been sucked out of its frail little body. The other was nowhere to be found. A weasel, we surmised, and after that we shooed them into a little house every evening after a day on the pond, they seemed relieve and often would be waiting for us to close the door.

A few days later I heard the mother duck quacking furiously. I ran over and waded through the reeds where I saw a duckling mostly submerged with just its head popping out of the water, peeping fearfully. I hesitated for a split second, visions of pulling my hand out with a weasel attached...then I plunged my hand into the murky water, grabbed what felt like a large pebble and pulled it up, flinging it way into the pond while with the other hand I pulled the sodden duckling, which I reunited to the grateful mother.

Two days later there were only eight. I walked the perimeter of the pond and saw the headless body of one of the ducklings. I bent over and pulled it out, the head had been bitten clean off, I quickly hid the little body under a rock at the side of the pond as I heard Iris yelling, "Papa what are you doing?" I called Bettina out of the house and by the time we rounded up the ducks there were seven another

had disappeared in a matter of seconds. I built a 500 square foot chicken wire duck resort and dug a small safe feeding to splash around in. The gaggle were miserable and would stand for days staring forlornly at the pond through the bars of their cage. Often they began to smell, they were messy, I read it in the books but duck poop smells truely bad.

Finally, after a week of scouring the pond for the evasive duck killer I caved in. Whatever had got to the ducks must have moved on and they were double the size, they were a weasel seriously. I let them out, I didn't make a big thing of it, no ticker tape parade down to the pond, no dancing neon finger pointing the way to a watery paradise, just quietly left the gate ajar. Twenty minutes later, enjoying my post-pig-feeding cup of tea I heard Iris scream, "the ducks have escaped!!" And there they were excitedly washing off a weeks worth of scum and poop quacking with delight

"They are fine," I said quite convincingly. "They are big now nothing can hurt them and we will lock them up every night." And they were fine for three days. On Wednesday evening I pulled my calf muscle, I heard/felt something pop and dropped to the floor like a ton of bricks. The next morning I was in the ER getting a temporary cast put on my leg, foot up for a week then crutches for two were the instructions. I drove to the lake and joined the family for a potluck birthday party and we all headed home merry. As soon as we pulled into the drive we could see something was wrong in the pond. The mother duck was spinning around flailing wildly as though pinned down, while the drake and the remaining seven ducklings

waddled nervously in circles up near the duck house. It seemed like hours passed as I hobbled towards the edge of the pond my brain trying to make some sense of what I was seeing then I heard a shout in my ear, "A giant snapping turtle has the mother duck! Save her!!"

I threw down my crutches and half hopped, half flew into the pond sinking waste deep into mud and slime. I battled towards the middle of the pond my leg screaming with agony as I reached the duck I looked into the face of a dustbin sized turtle. I screamed over my shoulder, "get me a fucking net, this thing is a monster," or something of the sort and I made a lunge for the duck. The dinosaur/Loch Ness monster sized me up and let go of the bird's spindly leg. I cradled the duck under one arm as I grabbed the net out of the air and thrashed it through the water desperately trying to catch the prehistoric beast. I ended up with a netful of algae and reeds and turned my attention to mother duck. Her right leg was stripped down to the bone and blood was dripping in a steady stream down my leg and into the pond. Back on dry land, we swaddled her in a towel and took stock of the damage. She was a goner.

The kids said their last good byes, and I took her behind the barn. After putting her to rest, I delicately and respectfully sliced her up and set two hooks and a raccoon trap within the meat. It's been a week and we still haven't caught the monster and quite forebodingly I found a baby snapping turtle perched on the waterfall yesterday. It is being held captive while I negotiate a ransom.

₃

₄

HOW TO
Write a Beer Recipe

BY
DAN SUAREZ X PHOTOGRAPHS BY
MARIO CAMILO

How to
Make Ricotta

By
DAVE GOULD

Photographs by
AARON WOJACK

₅

₆

Andrew Tarlow, Anna Dunn, August Heffner

DINER JOURNAL
Brooklyn, USA (Since 2006)

The *Diner Journal* is a quarterly publication that is independently produced and published by a group of restaurants and a butcher shop (Diner, Marlow & Sons, Roman's, and Marlow & Daughters). Together Andrew Tarlow, Anna Dunn, and August Heffner make themed journals with original literature, art, and recipes. All journals are ad-free and three-hole punched.

Photo: (1,4) Jeremy Liebman, (5) Mario Camilo, (6) Aaron Wojack, (p.118) Kate Huling and Andrew Tarlow
Additional credits: Publisher and owner of the restaurants and shop: Andrew Tarlow; Editor and chief and bartender at Diner: Anna Dunn; Artistic Director: August Heffner; All designs by August Heffner, (2) Article by Mark Firth, Illustration by Juliet Jacobson, (5) Article by Dan Suarez

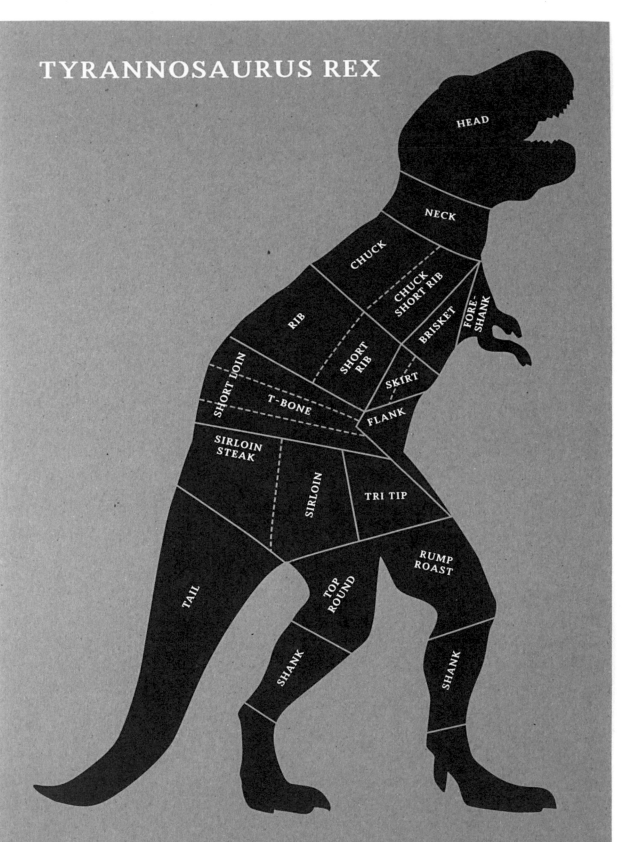

TYRANNOSAURUS REX

HEAD

NECK

CHUCK

CHUCK SHORT RIB

RIB

BRISKET

FORE-SHANK

SHORT RIB

SKIRT

SHORT LOIN

T-BONE

FLANK

SIRLOIN STEAK

SIRLOIN

TRI TIP

TAIL

TOP ROUND

RUMP ROAST

SHANK

SHANK

meatpaper   graphic by REBECCA MACRI
butchery consultant RYAN FARR

Sasha Wizansky

meatpaper
San Francisco, USA (since 2007)

meatpaper is a quarterly magazine about art and meat produced by Sasha Wizansky.

Left to right

meatpaper Issue 10

Photo: Julio Duffoo

meatpaper Issue 10

Illustration: Sasha Wizansky

meatpaper Issue 13

Illustration: Jessica Niello

Opposite page

T-rex poster
San Francisco, USA (2009)

This T-rex meat diagram was created for *meatpaper* Issue 9 and subsequently turned into a poster.

Illustration: Rebecca Macri

Chris Barton, Jessica Brent

Condiment — Adventures in Food and Form

Melbourne, Australia (since 2010)

Condiment — Adventures in Food and Form is a publication and project-base exploring the relationship between food and creativity and food and community. Published in Melbourne, Australia, by Chris Barton and Jessica Brent, it features a range of writing, photography, and essays.

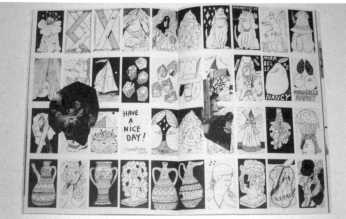

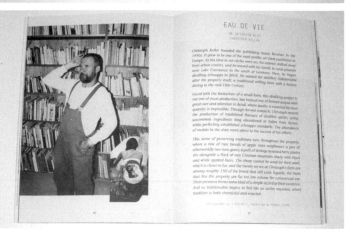

TONK
Taiyo Onorato, Nico Krebs

CONDIMENT — ADVENTURES
IN FOOD AND FORM

The Great Unreal

Taiyo Onorato and Nico Krebs
created the cover image for the first issue of
Condiment magazine.

Client: Condiment — Adventures in Food and Form

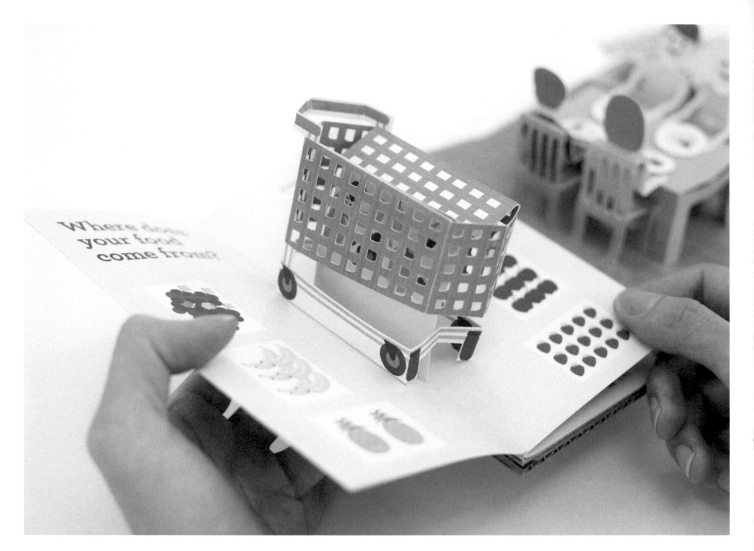

Adam Paterson, Santi Tonsukha

Grow Your Own
London, UK (2010)

Growing your own food is a great way to get deliciously fresh vegetables and take a positive step towards a healthier and more self-sufficient lifestyle. The book *Grow Your Own* by Adam Paterson and Santi Tonsukha contains all the practical information to get a garden started as well as the vegetable seeds needed. Produced as a pop-up book, its tone of voice approaches the topic of vegetable gardening and sustainable living in a fun way. Instead of telling people what to do, it gives them the information, knowhow, and tools to make more informed decisions about the global food supply chain and the vast distance that most food travels before its final destination.

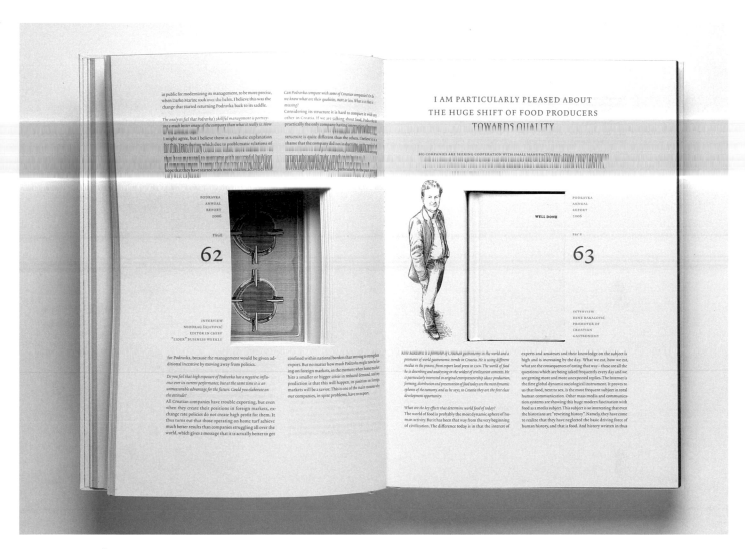

Bruketa & Žinić

Davor Bruketa, Nikola Žinić

Well Done

(2011)

The seventh Podravka annual report, designed by Bruketa & Žinić, brings together all three values of Podravka's brand— heart, warmth, and good recipes. This annual report has to be baked before use and consists of two parts: a book containing the numbers and report by an independent auditor and a small booklet that is inserted inside the book that contains great Podravka's recipes,

the very heart of Podravka as a brand. In order to cook like Podravka, you need to be a precise cook. That is why the small Podravka booklet is printed in invisible, thermo-reactive ink. Podravka's secrets are only revealed when its is covered in aluminum foil and baked for 25 minutes. If not precisely timed, the booklet will burn, just as any overcooked meal. If successfully baked, the empty pages will become filled with text and the illustrations with empty plates with food. To save energy, you can bake the book together with some delicious food.

Client: Podravka
Photo: Marin Topić, Domagoj Kunić
Additional credits: Art direction and design by Imelda Ramović, Mirel Hadžijusufović; Typography by Nikola Đurek; Account direction by Mirna Kapetanović; Production managing by Vesna Đurašin; Illustration by Tomislav Tomić; Production by IBL; Podravka, Project management by Drenislav Žekić

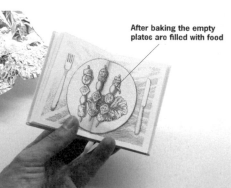

After baking the empty plates are filled with food

Martí Guixé

Food Designing
(2010)

Since 1995, Martí Guixé has been researching,
photographing, and designing food. _Food Design-
ing_ documents the work of this Spanish designer
and includes essays from various contributors as
well as photographs by Inga Knölke.

Photo: Inga Knölke

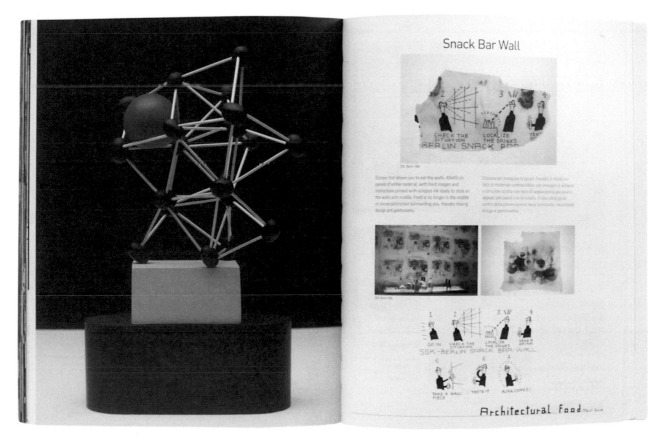

Snack Bar Wall

System that allows you to eat the walls. 40x40 cm panels of edible material, with food images and instructions printed with octopus ink ready to stick on the walls with nutella. Food is no longer in the middle of conversations but surrounding you, thereby mixing design and gastronomy.

Sistema per mangiare le pareti. Pannelli di 40x40 cm fatti di materiale commestibile, con immagini di alimenti e istruzioni scritte con nero di seppia pronte per essere appoggiate alle pareti con la nutella. Il cibo oltre a porsi centro della conversazione tiene le persone, mescolando design e gastronomia.

FOOD FOR THOUGHT

It is certainly no surprise that farmers, butchers, and chefs use food as their professional material—more unexpected is when artists and designers do the same. Food is used for its color, texture, and meaning by artists, illustrators, and photographers while clothing and industrial designers employ it to literally make their products or as part of their working process. Food proves to be extremely versatile however it is applied in these conceptual projects; its visual qualities can be manipulated to defy actual taste or render it unrecognizable and its cultural connotations can be compared and contrasted in cuisines and eating rituals from around the world. This flexibility makes food an understandable medium of choice for all disciplines.

Bompas & Parr

300 Dish Elizabethan Dessert Banquet
Kenilworth Castle, UK (2010)

Inspired by the majestic dessert banquet served
to Queen Elizabeth I at Kenilworth in 1575, Bompas
& Parr created an elaborate 300 dish dessert banquet in the castle's restored Elizabethan gardens.
Sugar sculptures of the garden's aviary, bear and
staff motif, and central fountain were created using an array of specially produced molds.

Photo: Ann Charlott Ommedal

Pages 130–131
Food Magic Kit
London, UK (2011)

Bompas & Parr created a food magic kit for Lyle's
Golden Syrup allowing anyone to create a spectacular food performance.

Client: Lyle's Golden Syrup
Photo: Nathan Pask

ARTISANAL CHEWING GUM FACTORY

Bompas & Parr

Artisanal Chewing Gum Factory
London, UK (2010)

Bompas & Parr built an artisanal chewing gum factory at Whiteleys Shopping Centre where visitors learned the secrets of chewing gum manufacturing at the world's first micro-factory. Each guest was able to choose and combine 200 familiar and unusual flavors including iris, white truffle, tonic, curry, and beer yeast; in total 40,000 flavor combinations were possible, including gums that changed flavor when chewed.

Photo: Ann Charlott Ommedal; Portrait of Sam Bompas and Harry Parr by Simon Jacobs

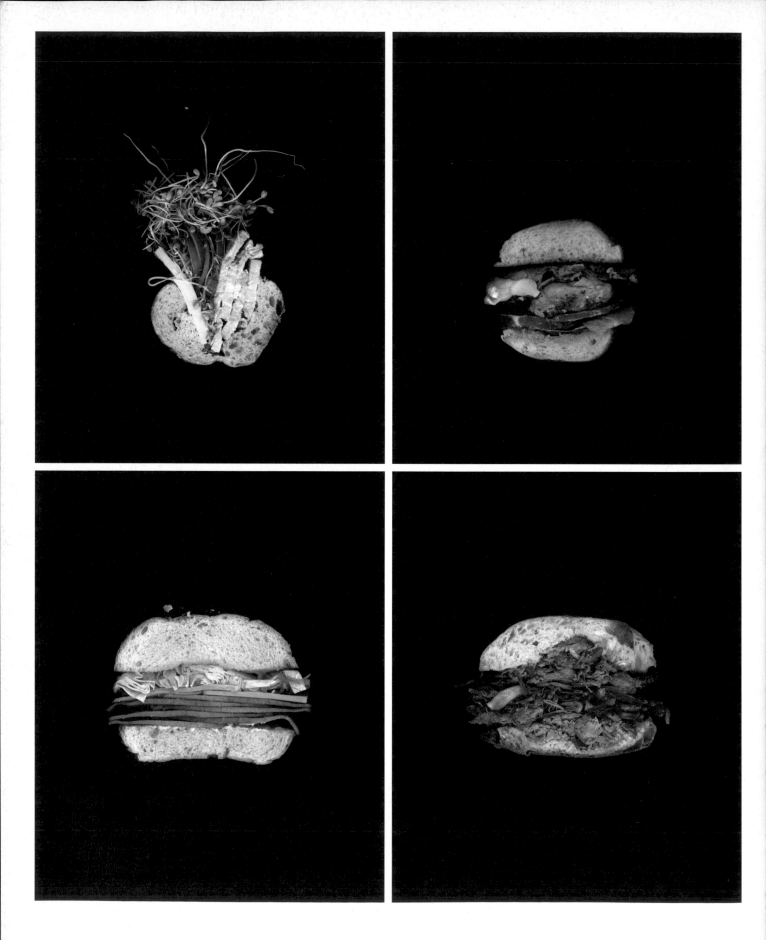

Jon Chonko

Scanwiches
New York, USA (2009)

Designer Jon Chonko scans sandwiches on a
flatbed scanner for education and delight.

Photo Jon Chonko

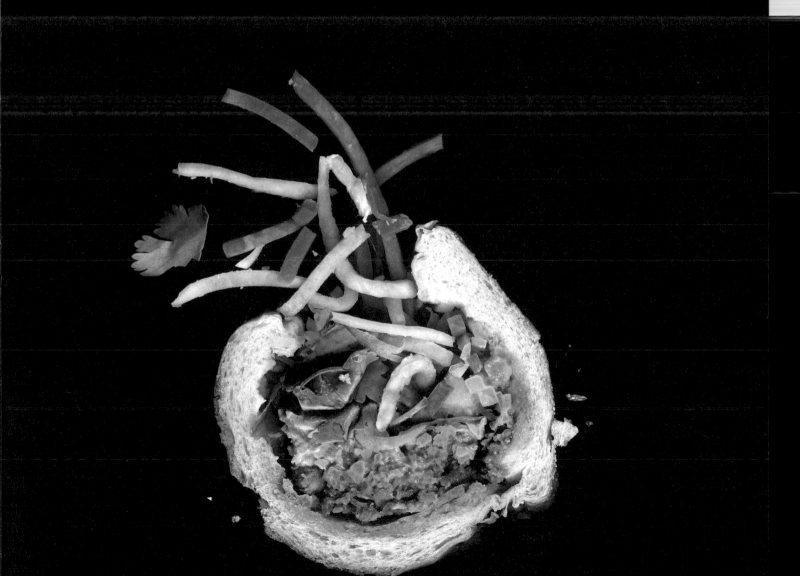

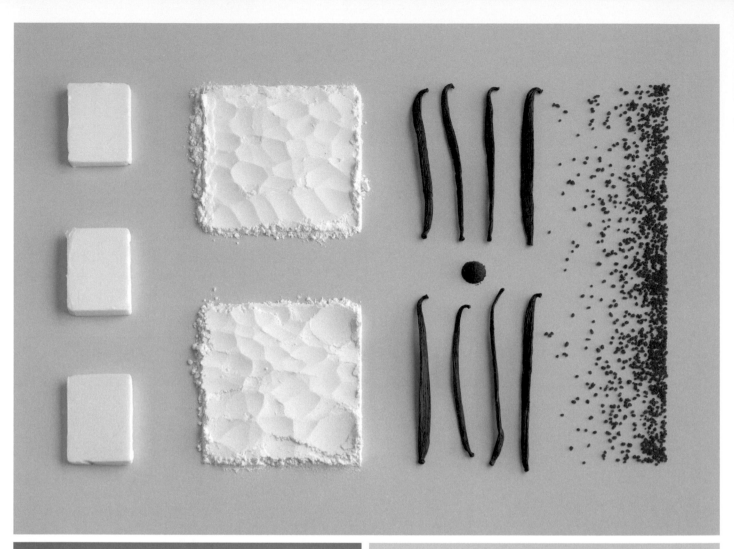

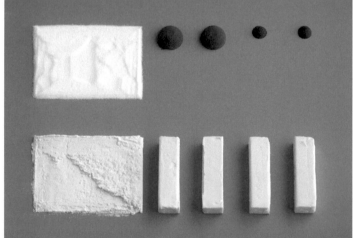

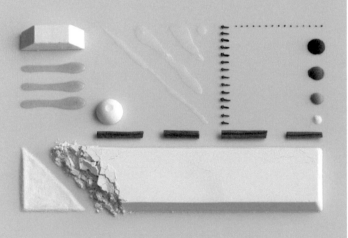

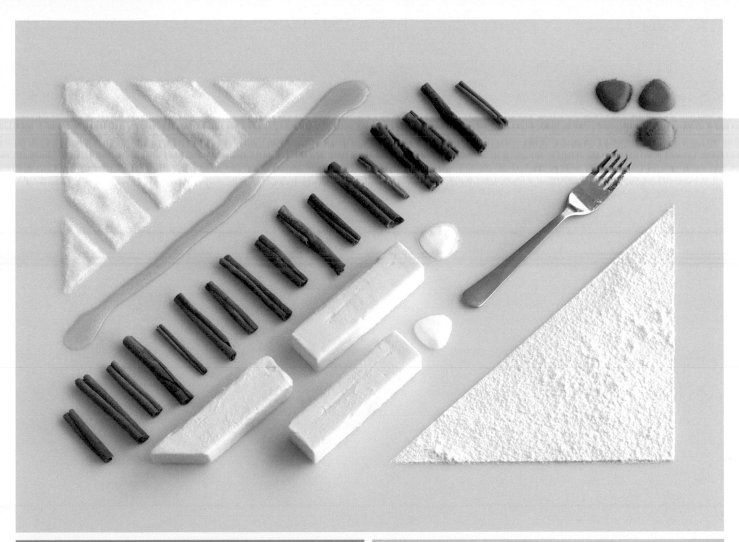

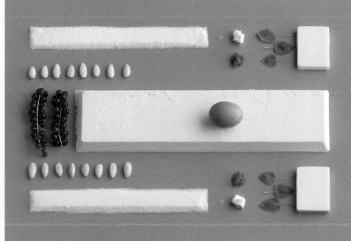

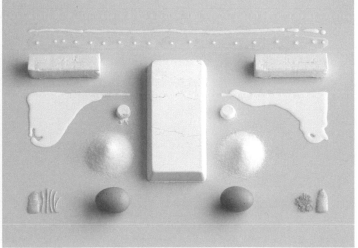

Carl Kleiner

EDITORIAL IMAGES FOR BLEND MAGAZINE

1 *A Paraphrase of Agnes Martin*
2 *A Paraphrase of Donald Judd*
3 *A Paraphrase of Frank Stella*
4 *Composition in Yellow*
5 *A Paraphrase of Kazimir Malevitj*
6 *Composition in Root Crop #1*
7 *Composition in Root Crop #2*
Stockholm, Sweden (2011)

Using only edible props such as rice noodles, linguine, fish, cheese, potatoes, and cabbage, photographer Carl Kleiner created editorial images for Blend magazine in collaboration with stylist Evelina Bratell.

Client: *Blend* magazine
Additional credits: In collaboration with Evelina Bratell

Previous spread
Carl Kleiner, Evelina Bratell

Homemade Is Best
Stockholm, Sweden (2010)

A baking book that contains 30 classic Swedish baking recipes for everything from small biscuits to large cakes. The photographs took an unusual approach to the subject, giving the ingredients the spotlight by photographing them in surprising compositions that draw attention to their colors and textures.

Client: Forsman & Bodenfors / IKEA
Photo: Retouch by F&B Factory

1

2 3

5

4

6

7

mischer'traxler

Reversed Volumes
Vienna, Austria (2010)

Reversed Volumes are bowls that are shaped by capturing the imprint of a fruit or vegetable with clay. After the original organic material is taken away, the bowl has preserved a detailed imprint of the food.

Client: FoodMarketo

IceDEA
Prima Chakrabandhu Na Ayudhya

Global Warming Ice Cream
Bangkok, Thailand (2008)

The assignment was to create an ice cream reflecting the global warming trend. The global warming effect was implied by creating a world-like ice cream with a swirl technique, then letting it melt, as if the world is melting.

Client: Cha-Muk-Mod (Thai television program)

Cocktail and Party Ice Cream Collection
Bangkok, Thailand (2004)

An event with a "party" concept prompted this cocktail and cigarette ice cream. Each flavor was served in a small cocktail glass or as finger food. The Marlboro ice cream was served in an ashtray, garnished with poppy seeds on the top.

Client: Red Box

Left
Grass Brownie for S-One Grand Opening
Bangkok, Thailand (2008)

The Grass Brownie is a special sweet created by IceDEA for the grand opening of a new football arena built with artificial grass. A dark brownie base represented soil and foi-thong, a thread-like Thai sweet, represented grass.

Photo: Courtesy of Bangkok Business Newspaper
Client: S-One Football Centre

Opposite page
Wallwafer* for Wallpaper*
Bangkok, Thailand (2010)

IceDEA's Wallwafer* was an edible design for Wallpaper*'s gastronomy issue. The wafer was chosen because its layers look similar to the edge of the magazine and because the word itself sounds similar to the word "paper."

Client: Wallpaper* Thailand
Photo: Image courtesy of Wallpaper* Thailand

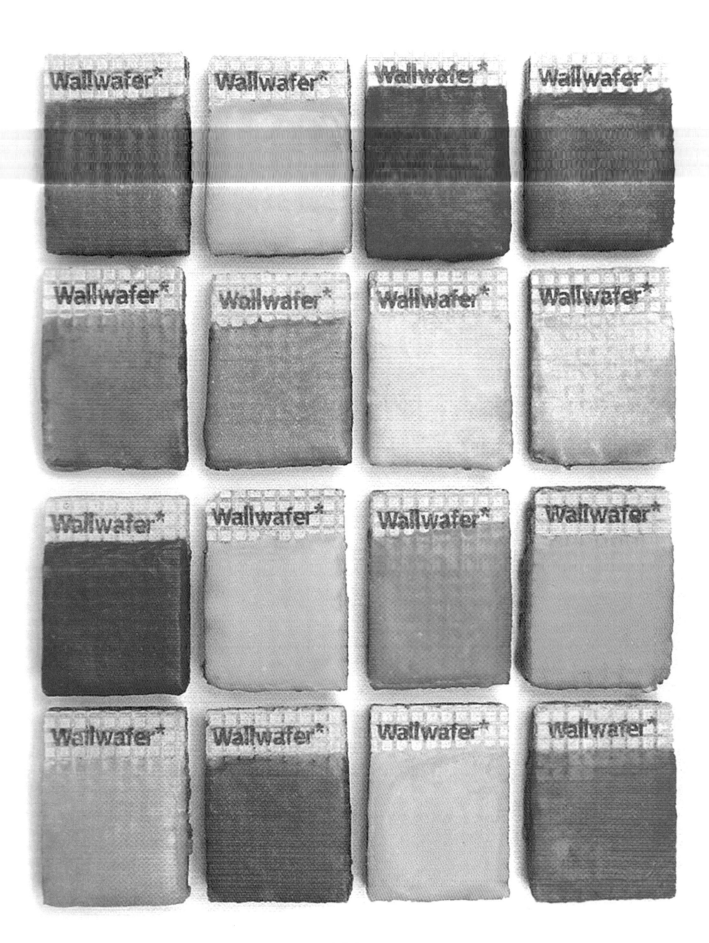

Jet City Gastrophysics

Jeth Rollins Odom
Seattle, USA (2010/2011)

Jet City Gastrophysics is a cooking group founded by Jeth Rollins Odom with the goal of cooking the dishes of the world's best restaurants at home. In doing so, the group hopes to explore the techniques of modernist cuisine — and demonstrate that it is possible for a home cook to produce high quality dishes.

Above
Pumpkin Oil Sweet

Malformed attempts to create the Pumpkin Oil Sweet by Ferran Adria from A Day At elBulli.

Above
Cucumber Chips

Component for Red Cabbage Gazpacho with Pommery Mustard Ice Cream by Heston Blumenthal from *The Fat Duck Cookbook*.

Left
Pea Meat

Leftover pellet of pea solids after a five hour spin in a centrifuge to create Pea Butter by Nathan Myhrvold from *Modernist Cuisine*.

Left
Ice Salad

Completed dish of salad and red wine vinaigrette by Grant Achatz, from the cookbook *Alinea*.

Photo: All images by
Jeth Rollins Odom

Shai Akram, Andrew Haythornthwaite

Chin Chin Laboratorists — Nitro Ice Cream Lab

Camden, London, UK (2010)

Shai Akram and Andrew Haythornthwaite were commissioned by Ahrash Akbari-Kalhur and Nyisha Weber to design the interior of their bespoke ice cream parlour. They wanted a space where customers could experience the making of the ice creams, which are frozen using liquid nitrogen. The rest of the space is an experimental kitchen dedicated to the development of modern confections. Each stage of the ice cream-making process is separated into its own workstation. The stations connect to form a self-contained, three-dimensional diagram of a nitrogen ice cream machine.

Client: Chin Chin Laboratorists
(Ahrash Akbari-Kalhur and Nyisha Weber)
Photo: Paul Denton

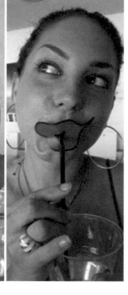

IceDEA
Prima Chakrabandhu Na Ayudhya & Fabrica

Fafi's Lips
Paris, France (2006)

French artist Fafi is a strong presence on the graffiti and art scene. Her images of sexy and liberated girls with playful pouts became the inspiration for these drinking straws used on the opening day of the Fafi exhibition File Dans Ta Chambre at Colette, Paris, in July 2006. The lips attach to the straws, inviting exhibition visitors to become a part of her drawings. When people drink from the straws, they appear to be live characters from Fafi's world.

Client: Colette

IceDEA
Prima Chakrabandhu Na Ayudhya

Frizzante Shopping
Paris, France (2006)

Frizzante Shopping is a new way of enjoying ice cream while shopping. It is an ice cream drink inspired by the way people shop in Colette, combining style, design, art, and food. The flavors are inspired by Italian cocktails, but made with ice cream and frizzante (sparking water): Spritz contains orange ice cream, Aperol, and orange soda; Sgroppino has lemon ice cream, vodka, and sweet soda; Bellini is peach ice cream, vodka, lemon soda caffe; Corretto contains coffee ice cream, grappa, milk, and caramel. The mixture creates a particular effect and texture and is served in a shopping bag-like container that makes it easy to carry while shopping.

Client: Fabrica

Marieke van der Bruggen

Top left

Candy Branch

Tokyo, Japan (2009)

The *Candy Branch* was an element of the installation *Garden of Delight* in collaboration with the candy shop papabubble in Tokyo.

Photo: Marieke van der Bruggen

Top right and below

Garden of Delight

The Garden of Delight is a suspended sculpture whose multicolored branches, twigs, and leaves come in different flavors that can be picked and eaten.

Client: papabubble Tokyo
Photo: Rene van der Hulst (top right); Mike Roelofs and Raoul Kramer (pooring hot candy in moulds)

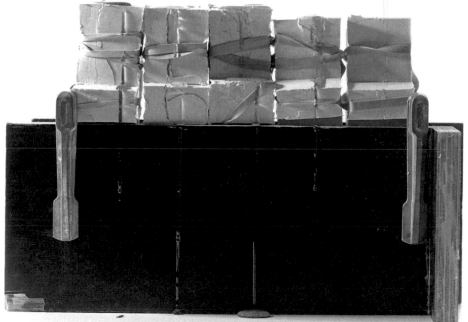

Eat & Art Taro

Ogori Cafe
Kashiwa City, Chiba, Japan (2008)

This project by Eat & Art Taro aims to provide customers with a new restaurant experience using a cash-on-delivery system; customers are served what the person ahead of them in line ordered. In turn, they place an order which will go to the person behind them in line. With this system, diners can only buy food for someone else. The Ogori Cafe takes its name from the Japanese word ogori, which means "to treat somebody else to food."

Client: UDCK (Urban Design Center Kashiwanoha)
Photo: EAT & ART TARO

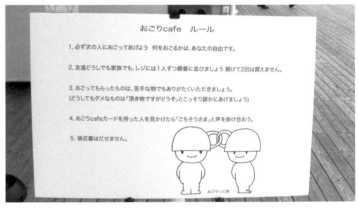

Martí Guixé, Antto Melasniemi, Lapin Kulta Beer

Lapin Kulta Solar Kitchen Restaurant
Barcelona, Spain and Berlin, Germany (2011)

It is well-known that solar kitchens use alternative energy: the sun. Yet it is not so widely known how the technical parameters of the solar kitchen affect food processing when cooking; taste and texture change in surprising ways, which brings about a completely different tasting experience. The Lapin Kulta Solar Kitchen Restaurant, created by Antto Melasniemi, Martí Guixé, and Lapin Kulta, is not completely dependent on sun for its food — it also serves salads and other foods that can be prepared with bright light and mild temperatures. This requires customers to be flexible; if it rains, a certain amount of adaptation, rescheduling, and dealing with delays must occur. The Lapin Kulta Solar Kitchen Restaurant is a business model that tries to rethink the perception of the kitchen, cooking, and food — all in relation to nature in 2011.

Photo: Inga Knölke

Above
MAEZM
Tai Ho Shin, Eun Whan Cho

Table-Dish-Cover
Seoul, South Korea (2008)

Spread the dishes on the table. This flexible table cloth looks just like a table of dishes and makes it possible to prepare food anywhere just by spreading it across a surface. The meal is over when the table-dish-cover is removed and washed. A sheet of flexible dishes that is folded or crushed brings a new way of life that is not affected by space or time limitations.

Photo: MAEZM

Above and left
DING3000
Sven Rudolph, Carsten Schelling, Ralf Webermann

JOIN
Hannover, Germany (2010)

Cutlery turns into cover. JOIN is more than simply a knife, fork, or spoon; it is a decoration for the table. The magic joining mechanism fascinates everybody, but not everyone will manage on their first try to transform the sculpture into cutlery — a little skill and a good eye is necessary. Do not worry — up until now no one has starved when unravelling the magic knot. In fact, many times a meal grew cold because the cutlery, made of high-tech plastic material, was simply too fascinating. JOIN was developed in co-operation with the BASF designfabrik™.

Client: Konstantin Slawinski — Housewarming Objects
Photo: DING3000

Olivia Decaris

Pouch
London, UK (2010)

Pouch is a malleable carafe that enables the
consumer to fill up a glass of beer and wine
by pulling and squeezing the container. Inspired
by a cow's udder and tension and suspension,
Pouch proposes an innovative way to serve, consume, and share drinks.

Dejana Kabiljo
FAT

Opposite page
Let Them Sit Cake!

This lounge installation *Let Them Sit Cake!* by Dejana Kabiljo paraphrases a quote commonly attributed to Marie Antoinette, but instead of ignoring the human condition by invoking the phrase, Kabiljo instead takes an optimistic approach and associates her work with Viennese pastry. Using nearly two tons of flour as well as 30 liters of chocolate icing, Kabiljo invites visitors to take a rest on an oversized cake in the shape of a sofa. Her work FAT is a soft suspended seat that references the other fine food of Antoinette's day — ham. All parts are reusable.

Photo: Studio images by Christian Maricic, other images by Francesco Troina

Olivia Decaris

Bang! Volcanic Bread
London, UK (2011)

Bang! Volcanic Bread was part of a culinary project commissioned by FoodMarketo for a dinner at the Barbican Centre in London. During the baking process, the volume of bread dough triples and its colors transform radically. The crust hardens, cracks, and browns while the inside becomes soft and elastic. Bang represents the incontrollable expansion of the dough that is similar to a volcanic eruption, dramatically recreating the contrast between the crust and the soft part of the bread. During the dinner, sixty Bangs with different flavors, such as tomato, oregano, poppies, and olives, will be distributed to the guests. The mold is milled and molded with FDA silicone, which controls the expansion of the crust and creates a series of similar geometric volcanoes. Duho is currently working with the Barbican restaurant on the development of the recipes and realization of the models.

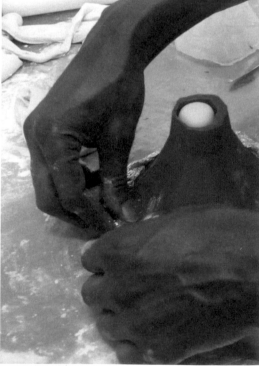

DesignMarketo

Dinner with DesignMarketo
London, UK (2011)

DesignMarketo teamed up with the Barbican Art Centre to create a shop within a shop, where a selection of products from their online shop as well as past events are available. The shop will also feature an ongoing set of design commissions in relationship with the gallery programming and exhibitions. To commemorate this collaboration, a dinner party was held at the Barbican Art Centre featuring specially commissioned recipes and objects produced by DesignMarketo's friends and collaborators.

Client: Barbican Art Centre
Photo: Amandine Alessandra for DesignMarketo

Borðið and Leir 7

Brynhildur Pálsdóttir, Guðfinna
Mjöll Magnúsdóttir, and
Sigríður Erla Guðmundsdóttir

The Claypot
Reykjavík and Stykkishólmur, Iceland (2008)

The primitive method of clay pot cooking
preserves more of a food's nutrients than other
cooking methods and inspired the creation of
the Claypot, which provides endless possibilities
for meat or vegetarian cuisines, bread baking,
and cake making. The Claypot represented
Iceland at the Berlin Nordic Bright Green Exhibition 2010 at DMY Berlin.

Photo: Valgarður Gíslason

Below

Hanna Wiesener,
Siren Elise Wilhelmsen
Client: Universität der Künste Berlin

(R)Evoluting Spoons
Bergen, Norway and Berlin, Germany (2008)

This project created spin-offs of the everyday
spoons including the soup spoon made of bread,
the whisk and spoon combination for cooking,
the camping spoon with a can opener, and
the spoon with a thermo chrome color to check
temperatures while eating or cooking.

Photo: Siren Elise Wilhelmsen

Poilâne
Apollonia Poilâne

Above
La Petite Cuillère Poilâne®
Paris, France (2007)

This spoon-shaped biscuit, designed by Apollonia
Poilâne, is the perfect partner for hot drinks.

Left
La Fourchette Poilâne
Paris, France (2010)

Apollonia Poilâne created this fork-shaped savory biscuit as an excuse to organize picnics and
cocktails.

Photo: Poilâne

Studio Formafantasma
Andrea Trimarchi, Simone Farresin

Autarchy
Eindhoven, Netherlands (2010)

Autarchy is an installation that proposes an au-
tonomous way of producing goods and outlines
a hypothetical scenario in which a community
embraces a self-inflicted embargo where nature
is personally cultivated, harvested, and processed
in order to feed and make tools to serve human
needs. A collection of functional and durable vessels and lamps, naturally baked at low temperatures, are produced with a bio-material composed
of 70% flour, 20% agricultural waste, and 10%
natural limestone. The grain Sorgho works as
a link between these crafts; in a perfect production process without waste, it is harvested and
used to create tools, vessels, and foods. Autarchy
suggests an alternative way of producing goods
in which inherited knowledge is used to find
sustainable and uncomplicated solutions.

Photo: All images by Studio Formafantasma

DUS Architects

City-Eyes Amsterdam Mugs
Amsterdam, Netherlands (2008)

For their Local Mug Project, Iittala worked with local designers in four European cities to reinterpret Kai Franck's Teema mug and encourage debate about the role of design in everyday life. DUS Architects, Iittala's Amsterdam partner, created two limited edition mugs for the project. The City-Eyes mug was inspired by the windows of the houses along Amsterdam's famous canals and the relationship they create between private and public space. The red crosses on the XXX mug were taken from the city's coat of arms.

Client: Iittala Helsinki
Photo: Elisa Sjelvgren

Yumiko Utsu

Condiment —
Adventures in Food and Form
Tokyo, Japan (2010)

The Japanese photographer Yumiko Utsu con-
tributed to the first issue of Condiment — Adventures in Food and Form. The publication — also
a project forum — investigates relationships
between food, creativity, and community.

Client: Condiment — Adventures in Food and Form

Arabeschi di Latte

Precious Waste

Florence, Italy (2010)

Arabeschi di Latte created a set of food presentation pieces for the Millefili stand at Pitti Immagine in Florence. The pieces were reclaimed pieces of porcelain that have fallen out of favor in everyday use.

Client: Patrizia Pepe
Photo: Arabeschi di Latte

Opposite page

Smarin

Stéphanie Marin

Mangier

Nice, France (2008)

This "tree to eat" was conceived in collaboration with chef Mauro Colagreco. Made of 100% beech wood, it is recyclable and eco-friendly.

Photo: Smarin

FoodMarketo

FoodMarketo is half pop-up store, half cooking workshop that sells contemporary design objects by upcoming and established international designers. Their daily workshops are a place to share recipes and everyday ingredients.

Initiator: Apartamento Magazine & DesignMarketo

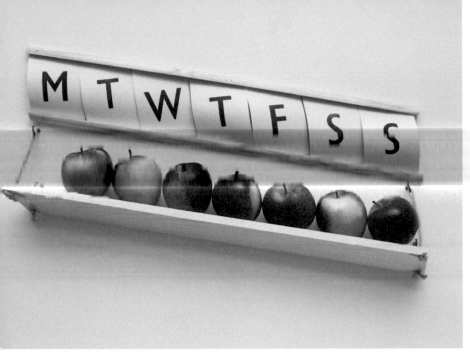

Left
Ken Kirton

An Apple A Day calendar
Milan, Italy (2010)

Photo: Amandine Alessandra for DesignMarketo

Below
Alexandre Bettler

The Bread Units:
A Day in the Life of Le Corbusier
London, UK (2009)

The Le Corbusier Bakes Units workshop was one of a series of events held in conjunction with the Le Corbusier - The Art of Architecture exhibit at the Barbican Art Gallery. Workshop participants used bread to find modular relationships between body parts in a process that referenced architecture and objects designed with human proportions in mind.

Client: Barbican Art Centre
Photo: Photos © Ladan Anoushfar 2009

Opposite page
Arabeschi di Latte

Workshop preparation
Milan, Italy (2010)

Photo: Amandine Alessandra for DesignMarketo

Left
Alexandre Bettler

Save Fish Eat Chips
Milan, Italy (2010)

Photo: Amandine Alessandra for DesignMarketo

Arabeschi di Latte

Made by — inflight meal

Milan, Italy (2011)

Arabeschi di Latte designed the *Made by — inflight meal* for the *Wallpaper* Handmade* exhibition in Milan. The project focused on people who make things with enthusiasm and a simple approach, becoming themselves the value of what they do. They arrived at the idea to create a homemade, inflight meal that resembled the people who prepared it; genuine, straightforward, and authentic in its ingredients and presentation. It became an intimate and physical reconnection between people, the things they consume, and the people who make them.

Client: *Wallpaper** magazine
Photo: Arabeschi di Latte

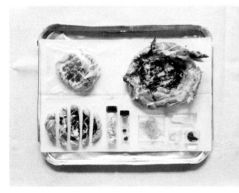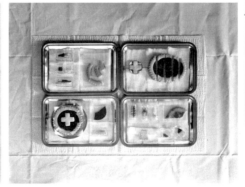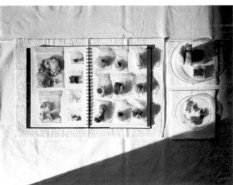

Kathryn Parker Almanas

PASTRY ANATOMY SERIES

Top to bottom, left to right

Confiserie Sprüngli I, 2006
Blueberry Danish, 2006
Confiserie Sprüngli II, 2006
Altes Cafe Schneider, 2006

New York, USA (2006)

Kathryn Parker Almanas's work uses food as a surrogate for the body and mortality. She began making photographs of anatomical dissections before using pastry to provide a connection to the visceral qualities of the interior of the body. Dissecting pastry provides a less obvious way of affecting the viewer's consciousness of their own body as well as carrying the themes of comfort and threat.

Kolle Rebbe / KOREFE

Food Finish
Hamburg, Germany (2010)

The Food Finish works just like finishing lacquer and is therefore sold in a classic spray can. A flow of consciousness variation on the themes of cooking and art is also used as typographic design element of the gold spray. The writing is intended to be inspirational and fun. Lovingly drawn illustrations take on this function on the cans.

Client: The Deli Garage
Photo: Ulrike Kirmse
Additional credits: Creative direction by Katrin Oeding; Art direction by Reginald Wagner; Copywriting by Till Grabsch, Gereon Klug, Thomas Völker; Account management by Kristina Wulf; Production by Produktionsbüro Romey von Malottky

Julie Rothhahn

Morceau
France (2010)

These sound cakes consist of vinyl in chocolate. The sound track is thought of as a sound ID card connected to an emotion and to the process of manufacturing the cake. Each cake expresses an emotion through its taste, color, and the sound that it produces— it really is records in chocolate that produce the sound. The cake presented here, a chocolate-brown biscuit and frozen Morello cherry espelette, expresses the emotion of anger.

Sound designer: Raphaëlle Latini
Client: Passerelle of Saint Brieuc
Photo: Julie Rothhahn

Sawa Tanaka

Edible Prints
London, UK (2007)

This series of screen prints on rice paper uses only food such as cream, flour, fruit juice, and food coloring.

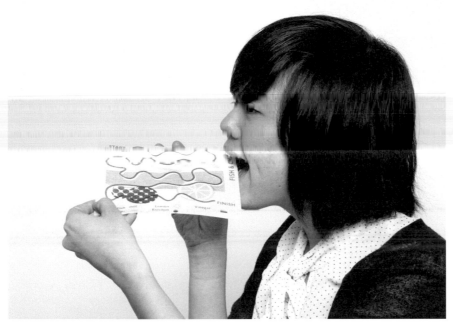

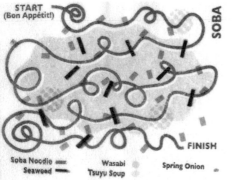

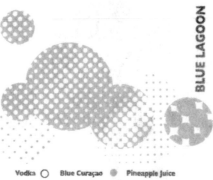

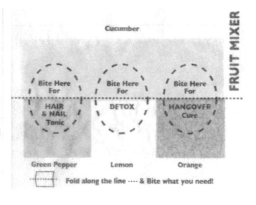

Louise Drubigny

Taking Apart the Clémanceau
France (2005)

The image used in _Taking Apart the Clémanceau_ is of the French aircraft carrier, Clémanceau. When it was too old to be in service, the French army had to take the carrier apart, but found the job too toxic for French workers, prompting them to ship it to India to be destroyed. The Indians worked without proper protection against the toxins, which turned into a scandal. This screen print by Louise Drubigny is printed on edible paper with food coloring and has a strong, bitter taste.

Tony Hornecker

Christmas at Number 42
London, UK (2009)

Christmas at Number 42 was a three-week restaurant/installation created by Tony Hornecker in the event space at the Architecture Foundation. Diners could make reservations to eat in one of the various rooms that were designed to look like the interiors of a modern home.

Client: Architecture Foundation
Photo: Daniel Hewitt

BLESS is a fashion label as well as an art collective. Founded in 1995 by Austrians Ines Kaag (who works from Berlin) and Desiree Heiss (who works from Paris), BLESS sits on the fine line between art object and design, high function, and high fashion. Their products are always unique and marked by the recycling and adaptation of unexpected items put to use in totally new ways. Their collections have featured edible clothes and accessories, including sweaters, tank tops, and sunglasses, in flavors such as coke and licorice. Inspired to change eating habits, they also designed cutlery and jewelry that makes the user consume food in new ways.

BLESS

N°42 PLÄDOYER DER JETZTZEIT
Paris, France and Berlin, Germany (2010)

The German title defines the BLESS state of mind. It is a plea for the here and now and the joy that comes along with being present. A limited number of edible garments, such as scoubidou gummy lace tank tops, knitted licorice, coke flavored sweaters, and lollipop glasses sweeten up the silhouettes.

Right
A group of models team-up in the Bloody Mary chain. Starting from a big cupboard where glasses are handed out, guests move from person to person getting one ingredient after another to build and flavor their drink.

Photo: BLESS

The Candytop, a lace tank top made of scoubidou gummy, can be worn — or eaten.

BLESS

N°42 PLÄDOYER DER JETZTZEIT
Paris, France and Berlin, Germany (2010)

Serverring

With the help of the Serverring, a ring that holds several small scoops of ice cream, an elegant way of eating ice cream is created; when in action, it appears that the ice cream eater is kissing their own hand.

Jeweled Eating Irons

With the intent of modifying eating habits, this cutlery is combined with jewelry that can be wrapped around the wrist for an elegant eating experience.

Candysunglasses

Lollipop sunglasses to be worn and eaten.

BLESS

<u>Nº07 LIVING ROOM CONQUERORS</u>
Tablecare
Paris, France and Berlin, Germany (1999)

The Tablecare comprises a piece of water-resistant fabric gripped by an embroidery frame; a tablecloth that can be used as a plate.

^{Photo:} All images by BLESS

Food Creation
Ayako Suwa

Pop / Pink / Blue
Tokyo, Japan (2010)

Conceptual food for the first anniversary party of Opening Ceremony Tokyo, an eight-level conceptual department store.

Client: Opening Ceremony Tokyo
Photo: Ayako Suwa, Food Creation

Opposite page

BLESS

N° 42 Plädoyer der Jetztzeit
Paris, France and Berlin, Germany (2010)

Somehow Related
Alison Thomson

The Chronic Facility
London, UK (2010)

One day there will be a health care service that caters to people living with chronic disease. Until that time, it must be imagined what it might be like to have such a service. The Chronic Facility is an alternative system for treating people with chronic diseases that is modeled after the restaurant industry and redesigned for this purpose. The project suggests a future outpatient department of the NHS with a holistic approach to health care. It provides a language for discussing issues of living with disease, as well as treatments and diagnosis. The facility uses representations of diagnoses created from food models made by scientists, which can then be served to customers. This speculative service has been designed from an inclusive methodology of workshops and performances that have resulted in the redesign of the relationship between patient, clinician, and scientist. This project was made in collaboration with the Neuroimmunology Group at Barts and The London NHS Trust.

Photo: Dan Medhurst; bottom line: stills from film by The Chronic Facility, 2010; Directed by Alison Thomson; Cinematography by Maja Zamojda

Jennifer Rubell

Creation
New York, USA (2009)

Creation was inspired by the first few chapters of Genesis, specifically the creation of the Garden of Eden, the creation of woman, and the expulsion and Fall. The installation location was chosen mainly for a use it no longer has: as the DIA Center for the Arts. This seemed appropriate for what is fundamentally a story of exile by choice. Each floor of the building hosts a series of food installations that people must interact with in order to have a meal. On the fourth floor are the drinking components: 3,600 glasses of varying sizes and shapes, one ton of ice cubes, 30 ice scoops mounted on the wall, a one-ton pile of roasted peanuts, and a pedestal of wine, liquor, and mixers in the 28-foot-long elevator. On the third floor are the savory meal components: one ton of barbe-cued ribs with honey dripping on them from a ceiling-mounted honey trap, five tables that each

seat 100, and groupings of water coolers, filled with red wine, white wine, and water. On the second floor are the dessert components: three felled apple trees with apples still on the branches; three nearly four-foot-cubed industrial bags filled with powdered sugar and cookies accompanied by shoulder length gloves to fish them out; hammers mounted on pedestals for destroying the seven chocolate facsimiles of Jeff Koons's *Rabbit* sculpture. The project as a whole serves many functions: as a commentary on the artisanal, the original, the unique, and the appropriated; as an exploration of ways to engage art history through a medium virtually absent from it; as a catalyst for a working interaction between viewers and objects — and viewers and each other; as a meal; and as a questioning of the boundary between art and all that exists to support it.

Client: Performa 09

Photo: This page & following spread: John Berens, opposite page: Kevin Tachman

BREAKING BREAD

Food events set themselves apart from both private dinner parties and restaurant dining experiences because of their temporality and conceptual intentions. Their creators often start with a theme and work from there. No part of the meal is too insignificant to incorporate into the experience: location, furniture, place settings, table decorations, the servers and their attire, as well as the guests themselves. That list doesn't even include the menu, whose ingredients are carefully chosen for their origins, connotations, and aesthetics. This overall attention to form and content makes food events feel like elaborate art installations rather than simply a good meal with a nice atmosphere — and that is the particular beauty in eating and drinking; both serve everyday needs but can also create one-of-a-kind experiences.

Marije Vogelzang

Sharing dinner
Tokyo, Japan (2008)

Sharing Dinner was created during the solo exhibition Eating and Design Part 2, What Design Can Do. The tablecloth, which covered the diners like a piece of clothing, made them all equal and allowed any participant to focus on the food and conversation rather than appearance.

Client: AXIS Gallery Tokio
Photo: Kenji Masunaga

Marije Vogelzang

Sharing Dinner
Tokyo, Japan (2008)

Sharing Dinner during solo exhibition Eating and Design Part 2, What Design Can Do

Place: AXIS Gallery Tokio
Photo: Kenji Masunaga

Page 186
Ham Man
Amsterdam, Netherlands (2007)

Inspired by the exhibition *Barcelona 1900* in Amsterdam's Van Gogh Museum, Marije Vogelzang created a Spanish ham tasting using a variety of traditional, high quality hams. Inspired by the idea of the *Gesamtkunstwerk* that was popular in the 1900s and intrigued by the sculptural quality of the work of the exhibited artists, she decided to make a ham man. Her inspiration was the Dutch annual flower parade where huge, flower-covered sculptures are dragged through the streets like a carnival. Building the statue and slicing the ham in front of the audience was part of the performance.

Client: Van Gogh Museum
Photo: Studio Marije Vogelzang

Bits & Bytes
Rotterdam, Netherlands (2010)

A dinner served on rolling plates for the opening of a Joep van Lieshout exhibition at Subma-
rine Wharf.

Client: Museum Boijmans van Beuningen

Marije Vogelzang

^{1,2} <u>Roots</u>
London, UK (2008)

While exploring the shared culinary history of
British and Dutch root vegetables, Marije Vogelzang discovered clay cooking, which enables one
to build sculptures, bake seasoned root vegetables,
and create a sensory landscape. In ancient times,
whole animals were baked in clay over an open
fire. After being removed from the hot coals, the
clay was smashed open. This project was an at-
tempt to connect past and present on a modern
table as if it were an eclectic archaeological site.

Client: Mintshop London

³ <u>Sur Place</u>
Amsterdam, Netherlands (2007)

For the Fortis *Sur Place* exhibition, Marije Vogelzang created a bread table covered in dough using
different types of bread connected to different
phases of life.

Client: Fortis
Photo: Marije Vogelzang

Left
Eating On The Beat
Gouda, Netherlands (2007)

A dish is a composition and tastes are musical
notes. Combining them and giving them space
and rhythm creates a musical piece in the mouth.
Directed by a big drum, the guests ate little bites
in a certain order.

Client: Krossin' Gouda Festival
Photo: Dik Nicolai, www.diknicolai.com

Below
Black Confetti
Rotterdam, Netherlands (2005)

An exact copy of wartime recipes served as little
snacks, which affected the memory of the people
who visited the exhibition. The bites released both
sad and fond memories and emotions.

Client: Historical Museum Het Schielandshuis
Photo: Studio Marije Vogelzang

Marije Vogelzang

Proef Restaurant
Amsterdam, Netherlands (2006)

A restaurant with simple food and a green
garden located in the best park in Amsterdam,
the Cultuurpark Westergasfabriek.

Photo: Alan Jensen

Jennifer Rubell

Reconciliation Dinner

National Portrait Gallery, Washington, USA (2009)

The *Reconciliation Dinner* was conceived to capture
the moment between disagreement and agree-
ment because the moment of reconciliation must
be harnessed at the very moment before it evapo-
rates, declines into war, or becomes too embar-
rassing or politically difficult to maintain.
The elements of the *Reconciliation Dinner* were
intentionally basic: a table of plywood boards,
wooden folding chairs, and generic tableware.
Decoration, luxury, and refinement were stripped
away. The bread was seen first — it was under-
stood that unless it was decided to break the bread
together, it would not be eaten. It was to be used
as a utensil, vehicle, and means of connection to
others. Bread cannot reconcile differences, but
it will bring people into a conversation in which
they can learn to give and to take and reconcile.

Photo: Courtesy of Jennifer Rubell

Tribe Studio

Eat Green Design Detail
Sydney, Australia (2009)

This project explored the conversion of a vast museum space into a pop-up restaurant. Forty guests were seated at one linear table, where they listened to a lecture on sustainability while they dined. The design intended to engage participants in the sustainability dialogue and create a playful space. The suspended plywood spirals reduced the intimidating grandeur of the hall, creating an intimate and inviting space by throwing a warm glow and interesting shadows onto the table. The installation was created from hoop pine plywood that was laser-cut and painted. The plywood panels were fixed to a fine steel frame and suspended on rigging. The use of the laser-cut tapering spiral involved extensive prototyping to achieve the right thickness of plywood. The spirals created an inverted mountainous topography and gave a three-dimensionality to the piece. Fabricating the panels offsite reduced the energy embodied in transportation, while laser-cutting and minimal use of materials allowed the panels to be transported flat. The ceiling installation was designed to be broken down into modules for wall art, trivets, Christmas trees, and table lamps after being dismantled. As it happened, the entire installation was subsequently bought by a restaurant and given a second life.

Client: Collaborate, the Powerhouse Museum
Photo: Murray Fredericks
Additional credits: Structural engineering by Damian Hadley; ISM Objectslighting by Simon Christopher

Prang Lerttaweewit,
Anders Mellbratt,
Josefin Vargö

Opposite page

<u>*Mixology 3: Composite Dinner*</u>
Stockholm, Sweden (2011)

A dinner was designed for the discussion about the future development of Telefonplan, the metro station and surrounding area that is home to the University College of Arts, Crafts and Design in Stockholm, Sweden. It aimed to answer the question: "What does Telefonplan taste like?" The dinner presented a stage where individual creativity morphed into collective knowledge.

Client: Konstfack University College of Arts, Crafts & Design
Photo: Anders Mellbratt

Above

<u>*Mixology 2: Don't play*</u>
Stockholm, Sweden (2010)

A dinner offered by a symposium about using play as a method says: "Don't play with your food!" The attendees entered Seminar Room 2 one by one, were granted a lab coat, a notepad, and a pen. That evening, researchers and practitioners were asked about how choices are made with curiosity, challenges, and playfulness.

Client: The Future of Play, Research Symposium
Photo: Anders Mellbratt

a razor, a shiny knife

NYC Dining Car
New York, USA (2011)

a razor, a shiny knife

NYC Dining Car
New York, USA (2011)

a razor, a shiny knife hosts educational, social, and theatrical culinary events around the world. This luncheon, held on the L line of the New York City subway, created a series of familiar gestures in commonplace locations using unfamiliar means. Serving a meal in such a dynamic and strained location presented a challenge that could only be overcome through teamwork and partnership.

Photo: Steph Goralnick

[snab] Society for Noble and Adequate Behaviour

Miriam Julius, Nils Lehmler

McDinner
Trier, Germany (2011)

[snab] is a gaming-community who keep records of their accomplishments in their fight against "global boring" on their website, www.snab.me. [snab] encourages players to interact with their everyday surroundings by taking on [snab] missions. The McDinner mission asked players to go against average dining behavior in fast food restaurants. Participants brought table linens, real silverware, and candles, which they used to set a formal table setting for their fast food candlelight dinner.

Additional credits: Intermediales Design, FH-Trier

Moritz Meyer-Buck

McDonalds Dinner
Berlin, Germany (2011)

A typical McDonald's customer enters the restaurant, orders some food, and sits down at a table by the window. They eat a burger, but not from the wrapper. Instead they prepare themselves for an enjoyable meal; fine porcelain, silver flatware, a small table cloth, and a candle holder are all arranged on the table. Coca-cola is poured from the paper cup into a wine glass. In a fine, candlelit atmosphere, the McDonald's customer finally enjoys their fast food.

Food creation
Ayako Suwa

Ayako Suwa creates edible artworks
under the name Food Creation. Her
work blends combinations of complicated ingredients with feelings and
emotions, serving up a visual delight
of sensuality and food that stimulates
not just the taste but all of the senses.

Below
Utopia food such as the a sandbank.
Tokyo, Japan （2006）

Conceptual food based on something in between artificial and real nature.

Client: Gallery Point
Photo: Ayako Suwa, Food Creation

Above
Food Guerilla
Tokyo, Japan （2006）

For the reception party of the Dafne Boggeri exhibition *I Started Something I Couldn't Finish.*

Client: Marios Left Tanker
Photo: Ayako Suwa, Food Creation

Opposite page
A taste of anxiety slowly blended with terror.
Tokyo, Japan （2008）

Editorial images created for the Japanese fashion magazine, *Numéro* Tokyo.

Client: Numéro Tokyo, No.17 (FUSOSHA)
Photo: FUSOSHA All Rights Reserved

Above
Trip food to 2027
Tokyo, Japan （2007）

Ayako Suwa created conceptual food based on a science fiction novel in which she imagined what people in 2027 might eat.

Client: Gallery Point
Photo: Ayako Suwa, Food Creation

Left
A lingering taste of regret with overtones of anger welling up.
Tokyo Japan （2008 ）

One in a series of edible works for the exhibition Sensuous Food, Emotional Taste that expressed human feelings and emotions with the combination of complicated tastes and forms.

Photo: Ayako Suwa, Food Creation

Food creation
Ayako Suwa

Eating Hibiya Park
Tokyo, Japan (2007)

Food creations for a party in the architectural
offices of Field Four Design Office, which are
located in a high-rise building by Hibiya Park.

Client: Field Four Design Office
Photo: Ayako Suwa, Food Creation

Opposite page
A taste of shame and joy that
slowly turns to pleasure.
Tokyo, Japan (2008)

Created for Ayako Suwa's solo exhibition Sensuous Food,
Emotional Taste held at the 21st Century Museum of Contemporary Art in Kanazawa, Japan.

Client: 21st Century Museum of Contemporary Art, Kanazawa
Photo: Ayako Suwa, Food Creation

Rachel Khoo

1 *Mash up II: Nature*
2 *Madmen*
London, UK and Paris, France (2009, 2010)

International food creative Rachel Khoo produces food-related events that mix thoughtful pairings of food with narrative styling. For an event at London's The Loft, she teamed up with illustrator T. Bass and sound artist Jay-P to create a delectable five-course mashup. The menu was inspired by everything in the garden including a pick-your-own crudité pot with potato pebbles and lemon aïoli and a frozen frog pandan mousse and multicolored frogspawn in a chilled Darjeeling tea pond. For a dinner inspired by the TV show *Madmen*, Khoo served New York cheesecake on New York City skyline plates, canapés of edible Lucky Strike cigarettes (mini grissini sticks) in ash tray hummus, black olive tapenade, and salsa romesco. Place mats were created from advertisements from the 1950s and 1960s and table linens were folded like suits.

Client: The Loft, My Little Paris
Photo: Kang Leong, www.photography.londoneater.com;
Additional credits: Illustrations by T. Baas; Sound design by Jay-P; Rachel Khoo

Rachel Khoo

La Petite Cuisine à Paris
Paris, France (2011)

British-born chef Rachel Khoo has organized and cooked for events and private parties all over the world — and written two cookbooks. When she found herself needing to test 120 new recipes for her third cookbook, *The Little Paris Kitchen*, she decided to open her apartment to the public. And so, in her own tiny Paris kitchen with only two gas burners and a mini-oven, she cooked seasonal, classic French dishes for two people at a time, twice a week.

Photo: Emilie Griottes www.griottes.fr

Ioli Sifakaki

Tantalus Dinner
South Kensington, London, UK (2009)

Ioli Sifakaki

Tantalus Dinner
South Kensington, London, UK (2009)

A different version of the Last Supper was created using custom ceramic tableware cast from
the artist's body. Twelve men were invited to sit
around the table and eat from these pieces. Ceramic objects are often related to rituals because
they resemble the purity and smoothness of
human flesh. Named after the mythic Greek king
Tantalus, who cut his son into pieces and offered
it to the gods, this project seeks to provoke new
relationships between the maker and the user.
The table had a torso shape and just as the body
was cut into pieces, the stools were cut as if they
came from the same piece of wood that the table
was made from. The vessels were filled with red
food and placed in random order on the table.
The guests had to eat everything without cutlery
before turning the pieces upside down and placing
each one in the right place to reconstruct the body.

Client: RCA for the final show
Photo: All images by Matthew Booth

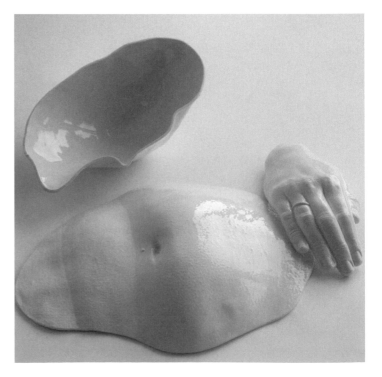

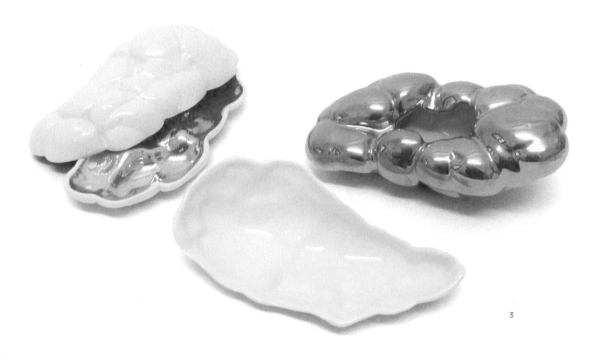

Marre Moerel Design Studio
Marre Moerel

FOOD ON THE TABLE COLLECTION

1 _Bomb water jugs_
2 _Testis salt/pepper shakers_
3 _Higado dishes_
Madrid, Spain (2011)

A collection of ceramic tableware consisting of jugs, plates, serving trays, and other related objects. Cast directly from animal organs such as cow hearts, pig intestines, sheep brains, and bull testicles, this process of immortalizing the animal's interior confronts the viewer with the brutality and animal instincts that also exist in humans as well as the beauty inherent in the rawness of nature.

Photo 1,3: Marre Moerel
Photo 2: Pablo Orcajo

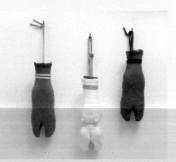

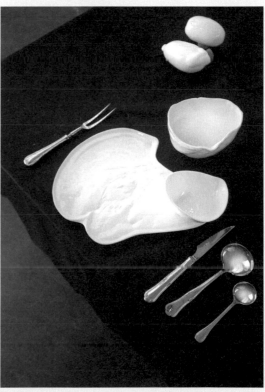

1   *Strung-Up Cow storage container*
2   *Bota Botijo water / wine jug*
3,4   *Food on the Table overview*
Madrid, Spain (2011)

Photo 1,2: Pablo Orcajo
Photo 3: Simone Barberis
Photo 4: Marre Moerel

HEL YES!
Antto Melasniemi, Mia Wallenius,
Klaus Haapaniemi

HEL YES! restaurant
London, UK (2010)

HEL YES! was a temporary restaurant and exhibition
conceived and realized by a creative team of Finnish
designers and food visionaries. Unveiled at the Lon-
donewcastle Depot in East London, *HEL YES!* served as
a melting pot of people and ideas for 14 days during The
London Design Festival 2010. A number of designers
came together to produce the furniture and accessories
used for the project: Linda Bergroth (round tables bent
from aspen trees); Alvar Aalto (Artek 403 chairs in three
new colors especially for *HEL YES!*); Harri Koskinen for
Iittala (lantern); Harri Koskinen Art Works for Iittala
(goblets); Timo Sarpaneva (cast iron casserole). The mix-
and-match plates were collected at the 2010 Iittala Plate
Swap dinner events in Helsinki, the open tents were
created with cashmere shawls from the Klaus Haapaniemi textile collection, and the kitchen was designed by
Linda Bergroth for Lapin Kulta.

Client: The Finnish Institute in London
Photo: All images by Adam Laycock

HEL YES!
Antto Melasniemi, Mia Wallenius,
Klaus Haapaniemi

HEL YES! restaurant
London, UK (2010)

Ryan Foote

Red and Yellow Event
Melbourne, Australia (2010)

Ryan Foote's recent work has focused on creating temporal events as works of art; he has created pop up bars and exclusive dinner parties, including a ten-course meal that consisted only of white food. The Red and Yellow Event consisted of ten unique hors d'oeuvres — five red and five yellow — such as beetroot crisps, cherry tomatoes covered with basil infused glaze on a red cream cheese base, red Champagne flavored macaroons, golden popcorn with a yellow salt, and yellow chocolate with charred salt and gold leaf. The singular colors stripped the food of visual taste signifiers and focused instead on the taste and texture.

Client: Exhibition at Platform Contemporary Art Spaces
Photo: David Cook

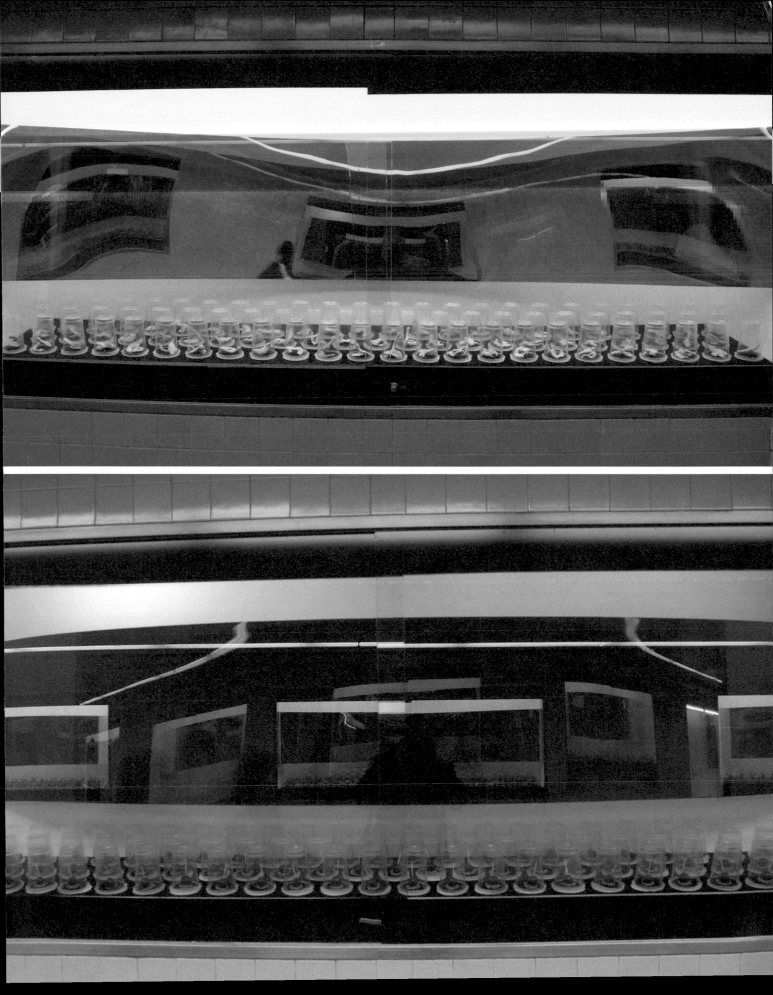

DUS Architects

Bardot Proviant Klub
Amsterdam, Netherlands (2010)

The exhibition *Bardot Proviant Klub* by Anya van Lit and Joost Bottema showcased Greenland's nature and culture as well as its changing environment and traditions. DUS Architects designed and built the polar dining room and table, where friends savored imported seal meat and other Inuit specialties. The walls of the room were shaped by one continuous sofa made out of pressed Styrofoam blocks, allowing all diners to share the same table as would happen during an Inuit dining ritual.

Client: Mediamatic
Photo: DUS

Below
DQM & Family Meal New York
Tashi Stricker, Chris Keeffe, Dale Talde, and Orland Delgado

DQM and Family Meal New York Presents Bodega
New York, USA (2011)

DQM partnered with Family Meal to transform the DQM offices and warehouse into a pop-up restaurant for a Family Meal. The concept was based on New York's unique type of corner store, where everything is for sale; the menu included Saltine crackers for a tuna melt, pastrami-style beef brisket, pork belly ramen served in a Styrofoam Cup of Noodles bowl, and chocolate tarts made with potato chips and pretzels.

Photo: Aaron Joseph
Additional credits: Design by Tashi Stricker and Chris Keeffe; Chef: Dale Talde

Arabeschi di Latte

Pretty Freaky Friday
(2010)

The Pretty Freaky Friday stops the perpetual motion of a long, hard week. A dress code gives way to a food kit that is casual. Saffron is the main ingredient for both food and drink. It is a panacea against anxiety, stress, and depression and awakens desires of all sorts. Saffron cocktails with rose petals were served in a bottle topped with a savory golden donut, and assembled with a pretty touch. Guaranteed to defuse tension and remind all that it is finally Friday.

Photo: Arabeschi di Latte

Arabeschi di Latte

It Takes Two to Tango
London, UK (2010)

Starting with the saying "It takes two to tango," Arabeschi di Latte introduced an interactive performance at the Victoria and Albert Museum in London that was a symbolic action inspired by heaven and hell. Dinner was served in a large pot with giant spoons intended for guests to feed one another and highlighting the importance of a collaborative attitude needed to solve big issues such as the global food system. *It Takes Two To Tango* was a reflection on solidarity through the opportunity for everyone to share a meal and prove their cooperative spirits.

Client: Victoria and Albert Museum with Designersblock
Photo: Arabeschi di Latte

DUS Architects

City-Eyes
Amsterdam Mugs
Amsterdam, Netherlands (2008)

To mark the launch of their Amsterdam City
Mugs for Iitalla's Local Mug Project, DUS Architects created temporary food performances in
Amsterdam. The city's windows, which inspired
their mug designs, prompted them to incorporate
windows into the events. The final food performance was held at the Iittala flagship store for
150 Amsterdam inhabitants; soup, ice, and bread
were prepared in the mugs and served directly to
the onlookers.

Client: Iittala Helsinki
Photo: Elisa Sjelvgren

Christoph Thetard

R2B2 — Kitchen Appliances with Alternative Driving Concept

Weimar, Germany (2010)

Using regenerative energy cannot solve the problem of electrical waste and the waste of resources. R2B2 is a set of kitchen machines powered by rotating a flywheel with muscular strength. The stored energy is used by connecting a kitchen machine such as a hand blender or a coffee mill, making electricity unnecessary. That means no electrical waste, less use of resources, independence from the power grid, and almost no noise while in use.

Credits: Graduation work

Postfossil

DMY Designer Dinner Schick-Nick

Berlin, Germany (2010)

Together with chef Till Bühlmann and supported
by the Swiss Embassy, design platform Postfossil developed the DMY Designer Dinner concept,
Schick Nick. Schick Nick is an active meeting
place, a mirror of cultures, and a new form of pic-
nic. It represents the design philosophy of both
Postfossil and Switzerland.

Client: DMY, Berlin & Swiss Embassy in Berlin
Photo: All images by Sonja Trabandt

Postfossil
Christine Birkhoven

Above

De Blanco for Trattoria Utopia
Ventura Lambrate, Milan, Italy (2011)

De Blanco is a series of porcelain cones that give
the user the freedom to choose their function: lying
down, the cones look market bags or fruit bowls;
when stood on end they look like tops; when put in
a glass, they appear to be vases for flowers.

Right

Madame Tutu for Trattoria Utopia
Ventura Lambrate, Milan, Italy (2011)

Madame Tutu can become either a stool or
household storage. The two contradicting materials, wicker and metal, are connected but can be
completely separated at any time.

Postfossil
Thomas Walde

Juri — 5 Forks on the Subject of Critical Design for Trattoria Utopia
Ventura Lambrate, Milan, Italy (2011)

With the extreme version of the five-part fork series, *5 Forks on the Subject of Critical Design for Trattoria Utopia*, it is impossible to skewer meat. The product stands for a vision of a meat-free diet in Europe. The Juri personal cutlery set addresses the controversial topic of meat eating. The fork contains one-fifth zinc and the knife is deliberately not polished, making eating meat difficult. The spoon's hand-embossed ladle fulfills the desire for careful hand-finishing; most of the handworking on the cutlery is visible.

Right
Juri — Personal Cutlery for Trattoria Utopia
Ventura Lambrate, Milan, Italy (2011)

In earlier times, people carried their own cutlery — usually only a knife — with them at all times. Due to increased mobility in contemporary society, personal cutlery makes sense because people often eat away from home.

Left
Juri — Cutlery Set for Trattoria Utopia
Ventura Lambrate, Milan, Italy (2011)

The Juri cutlery set addresses the topic of meat eating, controversial because of energy consumption issues. The fork contains one fifth zinc and the knife is deliberately not polished, which makes eating meat difficult. The spoon's hand-embossed ladle fulfills the desire for careful hand-finishing.

Photo: All images by Philipp Hänger, www.photography.philipp.haenger.ch

Postfossil

Trattoria Utopia

Ventura Lambrate, Milan, Italy (2011)

Postfossil set up its exhibition _Trattoria Utopia_ during the 2011 Milan Furniture Fair in Ventura Lambrate. The trattoria is a place where people from all ages and social circles meet, a melting pot and a metaphor for contemporary society. Though it may have different names, a form of the trattoria appears in most cultures. The _Trattoria Utopia_ collection ranges from cutlery, crockery, and seating to toys — all objects that can be found in a trattoria and that deal with the Postfossil vision.

Photo: Philipp Hänger, www.photography.philipp.haenger.ch

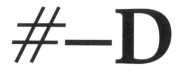

#–D

D–J

K–P

R–W

Delicate

New Food Culture

Edited by Robert Klanten, Sven Ehmann, Adeline Mollard, Kitty Bolhöfer
Text by Rebecca Silus

Cover and layout by Adeline Mollard for Gestalten
Cover photography (top to bottom): *Mangier* by Smarin, *TONGUES*
by Christiano Tekirdali, *La Petite Cuisine à Paris* by Emilie Griottes,
Homemade Is Best by Carl Kleiner & Evelina Bratell, *Proper BBQ* by Tom Hayes
Typefaces: Malaussène Translation by Laure Afchain,
Planeta by Dani Klauser
Foundry: www.gestaltenfonts.com

Project management by Rebekka Wangler for Gestalten
Production management by Vinzenz Geppert for Gestalten
Proofreading by transparent Language Solutions
Printed by optimal media Production, Röbel
Made in Germany

Published by Gestalten, Berlin 2011
ISBN 978-3-89955-369-7

None of the content in this book was published in exchange
for payment by commercial parties or designers; Gestalten
selected all included work based solely on its artistic merit.

This book was printed on paper certified by the FSC®.

Gestalten is a climate-neutral company. We collaborate
with the non-profit carbon offset provider myclimate
(www.myclimate.org) to neutralize the company's carbon
footprint produced through our worldwide business activities
by investing in projects that reduce CO_2 emissions
(www.gestalten.com/myclimate).

myclimate
Protect our planet

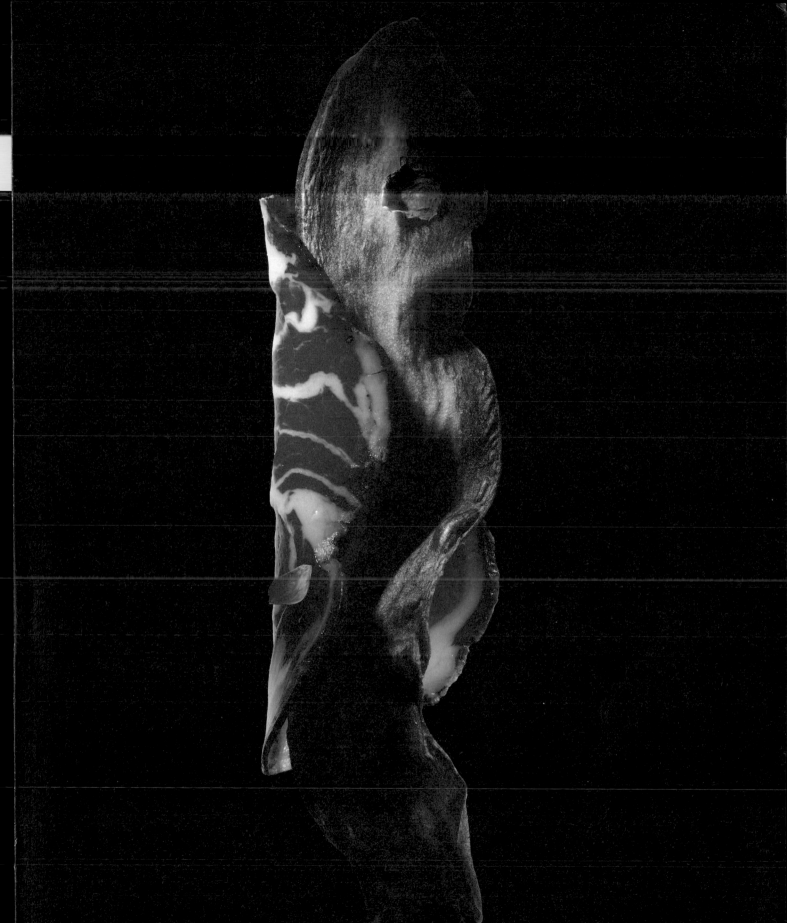